Ready-Made ters

for Differenti ... ction

Grade 1

Scott Foresman·Addison Wesley

enVisionMATH®
Common Core

PEARSON

Glenview, Illinois • Boston, Massachusetts • Chandler, Arizona • Upper Saddle River, New Jersey

ISBN-13: 978-0-328-81053-6
ISBN-10: 0-328-81053-3

1 2 3 4 5 6 7 8 9 10 V0SI 18 17 16 15 14

Grade 1 Topic Titles

Common Core

Standards for Mathematical Content

Domain: Operations and Algebraic Thinking
Topics: 1, 2, 3, 4, 5, and 6

Domain: Number and Operations in Base Ten
Topics: 7, 8, 9, 10 and 11

Domain: Measurement and Data
Topics: 12, 13, and 14

Domain: Geometry
Topics: 15 and 16

Standards for Mathematical Practice

- ✔ Make sense of problems and persevere in solving them.
- ✔ Reason abstractly and quantitatively.
- ✔ Construct viable arguments and critique the reasoning of others.
- ✔ Model with mathematics.
- ✔ Use appropriate tools strategically.
- ✔ Attend to precision.
- ✔ Look for and make use of structure.
- ✔ Look for and express regularity in repeated reasoning.

Domain: Operations and Algebraic Thinking

Topic **1** Understanding Addition

Topic **2** Understanding Subtraction

Topic **3** Five and Ten Relationships

Topic **4** Addition and Subtraction Facts to 12

Topic **5** Addition Facts to 20

Topic **6** Subtraction Facts to 20

Domain: Number and Operations in Base Ten

Topic **7** Counting and Number Patterns to 120

Topic **8** Tens and Ones

Topic **9** Comparing Numbers to 100

Topic **10** Adding with Tens and Ones

Topic **11** Subtracting with Tens and Ones

Domain: Measurement and Data

Topic **12** Length

Topic **13** Time

Topic **14** Using Data to Answer Questions

Domain: Geometry

Topic **15** Geometry

Topic **16** Fractions of Shapes

Ready-Made Centers
for Differentiated Instruction

1 Each of the 5 spiral-bound books in the box contains an on-level, one-star activity, and an advanced-level, two-star activity, for every lesson.

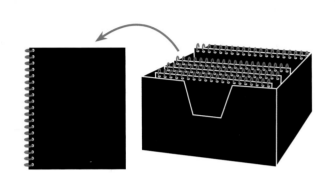

One-star activity   **Two-star activity**

2 Manipulatives

20 number cubes

100 red and 100 blue square tiles

10 sets of number tiles (0-9)

3 Plastic Bags:

5 plastic bags

4 School-supplied items:

20 large paper clips

35 small paper clips

5 paper lunch bags

1 Divide all materials equally into the 5 plastic bags.

20 red square tiles

20 blue square tiles

2 sets of number tiles (0-9)

7 small paper clips

4 large paper clips

4 number cubes

2 Store the activity materials in the front section of the box.

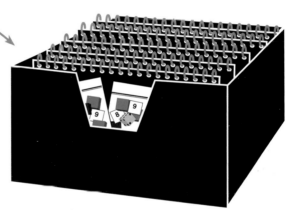

"Grab and Go"

- Each group of students doing an activity grabs a book, a plastic bag of manipulatives, and (if needed) a paper bag. Groups then work independently to complete one or both leveled activities.

- Occasionally, manipulatives and/or Teaching Tool masters used during the lesson will also be needed to complete the Center Activities.

- When students complete an activity, they return the book and the bag of manipulatives to the box.

Try Together

Partner Talk
Share your thinking while you work.

Start 🧍 Put `0` `1` `2` `3` `4` `5` in a 🛍️.

Get 5 red squares for one partner.
Get 5 blue squares for the other partner.
Work together.

Try Pick a tile. Put that number of squares on the workmat. Have a partner put some squares on the other side of the workmat. Count to find how many squares there are in all. Remove your squares. Repeat until the 🛍️ is empty.

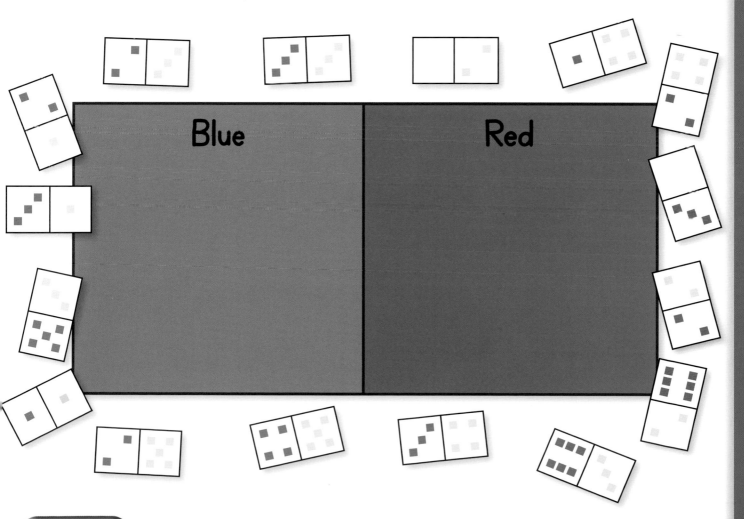

Blue   Red

Try Again Work together. Use counters to show 10 two different ways.

Try Together

Start Put  in a 🛍.

Get 5 red squares for one partner.
Get 5 blue squares for the other partner.
Work together.

Try Pick a tile. Show that number on the workmat using red and blue squares. Then use a **different number of squares** to show the same number.

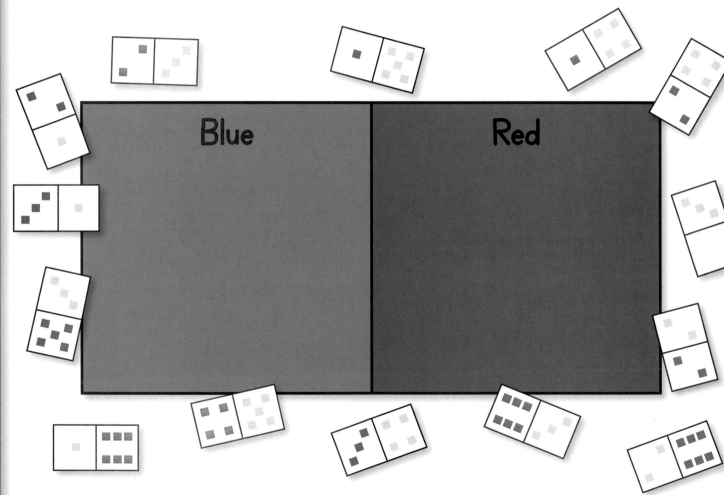

Repeat until the 🛍 is empty.

Try Again Find nine different ways to show 10 with counters.

Try Together

Partner Talk

Share your thinking while you work.

Start  Put ⬚1⬚ ⬚2⬚ ⬚3⬚ ⬚4⬚ ⬚5⬚ ⬚6⬚ in a .

Get 7 red squares for one player.
Get 7 blue squares for the other player. Take turns.

Try Pick a tile. Show that number of red squares on the beach balls.
Do you have 6 squares in all? If not, put blue squares
on other balls until there are 6 squares in all.

Ask your partner to say: _____ red _____ blue _____ in all.

Keep the tile. Remove your squares. Take turns until the is empty.

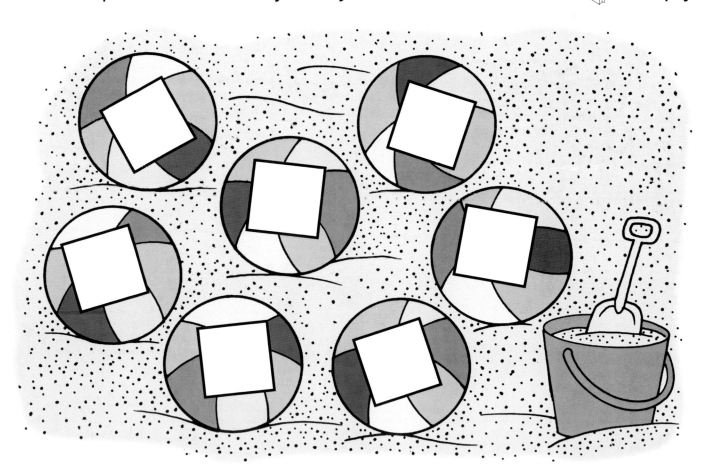

Try Again This time, put squares on 7 balls.
Talk about what "in all" means.

Center Activity 1-2

Try Together

Start 👫 Put [6] [6] [7] [7] in a 🛍.

Get 10 red squares for one player.
Get 10 blue squares for the other player. Take turns.

Try Pick a tile. Look for a beach ball with parts of that number.
If you find one, clap the two parts of your number.
Then put a square on that ball. Put the tile back in the 🛍.
Play until all the balls are covered.

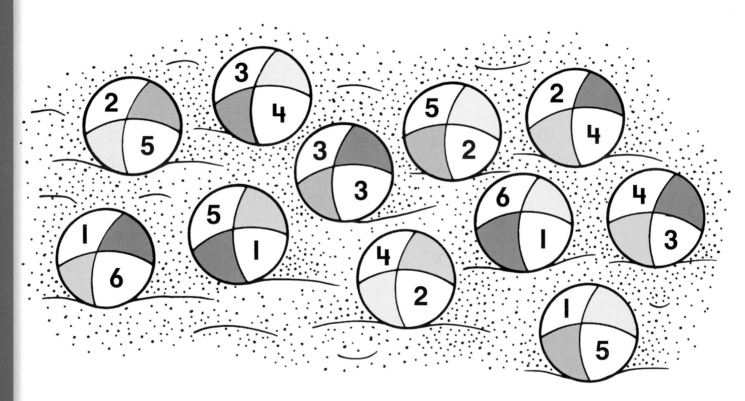

To win, cover the most balls.

Try Again This time, you can cover one or two balls on your turn.
Talk about how the ball with 3 and 3 is different from
the others.

Center Activity ★ ★ **1-2**

Partner Talk
Share your thinking while you work.

Start Get 20 red squares for one player.
Get 20 blue squares for the other player.
Get 🎲 🎲. Take turns.

Try Toss the 🎲 🎲. Say each number of dots.

IF YOU SAY	COVER THE PATH WITH
2 and 6	▪
3 and 5	▪ ▪
4 and 4	▪ ▪ ▪

If you say
other numbers,
miss a turn.

Start Here!

Cover the Path!

To win, put the most squares on the path!

Try Again Play again!

Play a Game

Start Get 20 red squares for one player.
Get 20 blue squares for the other player.
Get . Take turns.

Try Toss the . Say each number of dots.

IF YOU SAY	COVER THE PATH WITH
2 and 6	■
3 and 5	■ ■
4 and 4	■ ■ ■

If you say
other numbers,
miss a turn.

Start Here! ↓

Cover the Path!

	Count from 8 to 0.
Clap 8 times.	
	Move ahead 1 space.
Count to 8.	Stomp 8 times.
	Move ahead 1 space.

To win, put the most squares on the path!

	Move ahead 1 space.		Blink 8 times.		

Try Again Play again! If you toss one dot, can you get the
other part of 8 on the second cube?

Partner Talk

Share your thinking while you work.

Cover Three

Start Put  in a 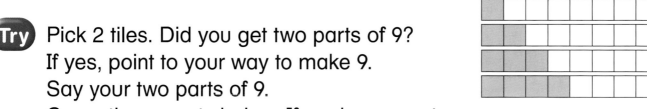.

Get 6 red squares for one player.
Get 6 blue squares for the other player.
Take turns.

Ways to Make 9

Try Pick 2 tiles. Did you get two parts of 9?
If yes, point to your way to make 9.
Say your two parts of 9.
Cover those parts below. If no, lose your turn.
Put the tiles back in the.

3 and 6	4 and 5	8 and 1
1 and 8	7 and 2	5 and 4
2 and 7	6 and 3	1 and 8

To win, get: ■ ■ ■ or ■ or ■   or   ■

Try Again Play again!

Cover Three

Start Put 1 2 3 4 5 6 7 8 in a bag.

Get 6 red squares for one player.
Get 6 blue squares for the other player.
Take turns.

Try Pick one tile. Touch that number of rectangles on the game board.
How many more rectangles do you need to get 9 in all?
Pick another tile. Did you get the other part of 9?
If yes, cover those two parts to make 9. If no, lose your turn.
Put the tiles back in the bag.

5 and 4	7 and 2	6 and 3
6 and 3	1 and 8	4 and 5
2 and 7	3 and 6	8 and 1

To win, get: ■■■ or ■ or ■ or ■
               ■   ■   ■
               ■   ■   ■

Try Again Can one part of 9 be greater than 9? Play again!

Helping Hands

Start  Put  in a .

Work together.

Try Pick a tile. Put that number of your fingers on one hand below. Let your partner pick a tile. Your partner shows that number of fingers on the other hand.

Say: _____ and _____ is _____ in all.

Trace the numbers and the signs for your addition sentence in the air.

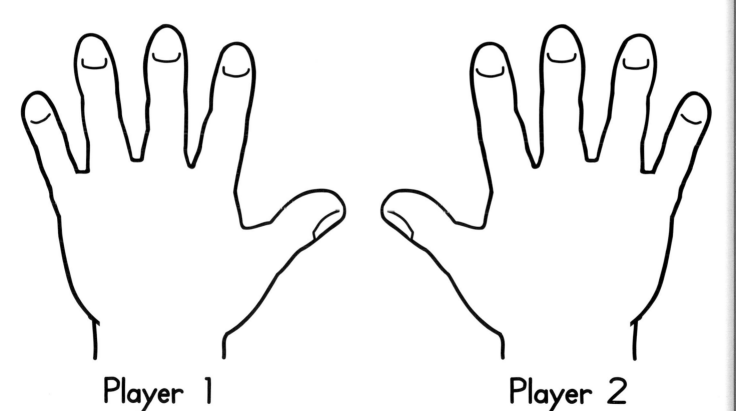

Player 1   Player 2

Try Again Put the tiles back in the 🛍. Repeat.
This time, say: _____ plus _____ equals _____ .

Center Activity ★ 1-5

Helping Hands

Start Put 5 red squares and 5 blue squares in a . Take turns.

Try Pick a handful of squares. Use the workmat to sort the squares.

Say: _____ and _____ is _____ in all.

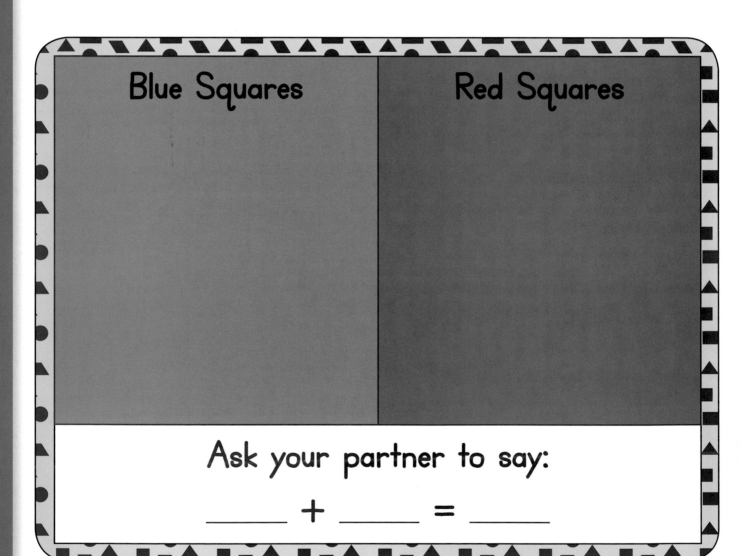

Blue Squares   Red Squares

Ask your partner to say:

_____ **+** _____ **=** _____

Try Again Put the squares back in the . Repeat.
This time, put 6 red squares and 6 blue squares in the.

Center Activity ★ ★ **1-5**

Play a Game

Partner Talk

Share your thinking while you work.

Start  Put ⒈ ② ③ ④ ⑤ ⑥ ⑦ ⑧ in a 🛍.

Get 18 red squares.
Give one game board to each player. Take turns.

Try Pick a tile. Tell a story about joining that number with 2.
Any player who has the number in all covers that sum.
Put the tile back in the 🛍. Repeat until one player wins.

Four Corners		
3	5	7
8	6	9
10	3	4

Four Corners		
9	4	5
10	3	7
6	4	8

To win, be the first player to cover four corners.

Try Again Play again!

Play a Game

Partner Talk

Share your thinking while you work.

Start 🏃 Put  1 2 3 4 5 6 7 8 in a .

Get 18 red squares.
Give one game board to each player. Take turns.

Try Pick a tile. Each player points to that number of cats.
How many cats joined with those to make 10 in all?
Any player who has the answer covers that number.
Put the tile back in the 🛍. Repeat until one player wins.

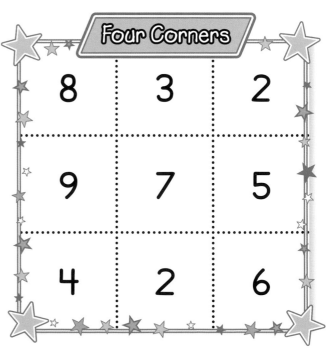

Four Corners

3	4	5
9	8	6
7	2	4

Four Corners

8	3	2
9	7	5
4	2	6

To win, be the first player to cover four corners.

Try Again Play again!

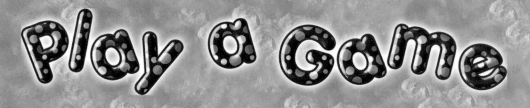

Partner Talk

Share your thinking while you work.

Start 👬 Get 12 red squares.
Cover each game space with a square. Take turns.

Try Uncover two game spaces. Did you find two facts that have the same numbers in a different order?

If **YES**, say the sum for those numbers. Keep the squares.

If **NO**, put the squares back where they were.

Take turns until all the spaces are uncovered.

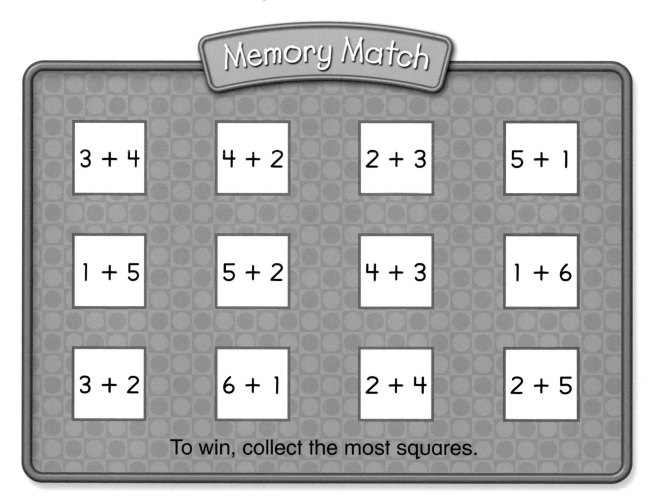

Memory Match

3 + 4	4 + 2	2 + 3	5 + 1
1 + 5	5 + 2	4 + 3	1 + 6
3 + 2	6 + 1	2 + 4	2 + 5

To win, collect the most squares.

Try Again Play again!

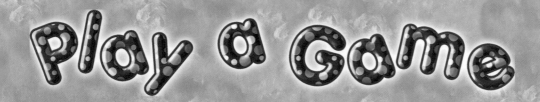

Partner Talk

Share your thinking while you work.

Start  Get two 🎲 🎲.
Get 20 red squares for one player.
Get 20 blue squares for the other player. Take turns.

Try Toss 🎲 🎲. Toss again if your two numbers are the same.

If two game spaces have numbers that match the numbers on the cubes, say the sum. Cover those spaces.

If not, lose your turn.

Play until one player covers six game spaces.

Memory Match

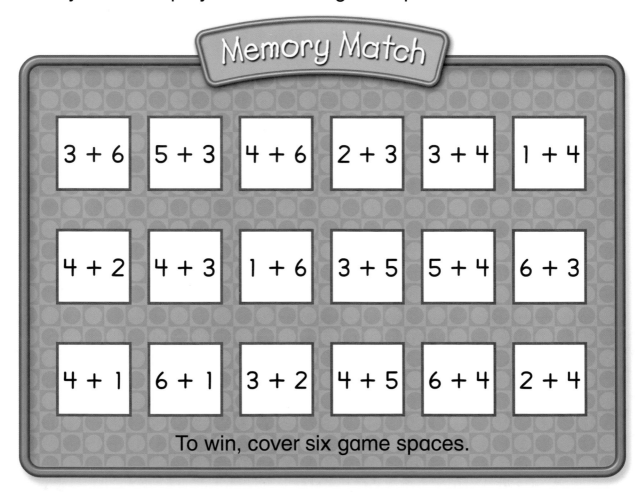

3 + 6	5 + 3	4 + 6	2 + 3	3 + 4	1 + 4
4 + 2	4 + 3	1 + 6	3 + 5	5 + 4	6 + 3
4 + 1	6 + 1	3 + 2	4 + 5	6 + 4	2 + 4

To win, cover six game spaces.

Try Again Play again!

Helping Hands

Start Put  6 7 8 9 in a .

Get 9 red squares. Pretend your squares are tickets.
Take turns until each player gets 5 turns.

Try Pick a tile. Count that number of tickets.
Explain how to spend that number of tickets on 2 things at
the amusement park. Put the tile back in the .

2 tickets

2 tickets

5 tickets

5 tickets

4 tickets

3 tickets

4 tickets

3 tickets

1 ticket

4 tickets

6 tickets

Try Again Choose two or three things you would like to ride or buy at
the amusement park. Tell how many tickets you need in all.

Helping Hands

Partner Talk
Share your thinking while you work.

Start Put 6 7 8 9 in a bag.

Get 9 red squares. Pretend your squares are tickets.
Take turns until each player gets 5 turns.

Try Pick a tile. Count that number of tickets. Explain how to spend that number of tickets on 2 things at the amusement park.
Then find a different way to spend all of your tickets on 2 things.
Put the tile back in the bag.

2 tickets

2 tickets

5 tickets

5 tickets

4 tickets

3 tickets

4 tickets

3 tickets

1 ticket

4 tickets

6 tickets

Try Again This time, use your tickets to buy 3 things.

Start Count 6 red squares with your partner. Put them in a ⬜. Take turns.

Try Take some squares from the ⬜. Show your partner.
Count those squares.
Ask your partner how many squares are left in the ⬜.
Check your partner's answer.
Count the squares left in the ⬜.
Put the squares back in the ⬜.
Repeat until each player gets 3 turns.

Count your squares here.

Try Again Begin again. This time, put 7 squares in the ⬜.

Partner Talk

Share your thinking while you work.

Try Together

Start 🏃 Count 7 red squares with your partner. Put them in a 🛍. Take turns.

Try Take some squares from the 🛍.
Clap that number of times.
Ask your partner to clap the missing number.
Check by counting the squares left in the 🛍.
Put the squares back in the 🛍.
Repeat until each player gets 4 turns.

Count your squares here.

Try Again Begin again. This time, put fewer than 7 squares in the 🛍.
Talk about how you find the missing part.

Center Activity ★ ★ **2-1**

Play a Game

Partner Talk
Share your thinking while you work.

Start 👫 Count 8 blue squares with your partner. Put them in a 🛍. Get 18 red squares. Give one game board to each player. Play at the same time.

Try Take some squares from the 🛍. Count them. How many squares are still in the 🛍? Check your answer by counting. Look on your game board for the number of squares left in the 🛍. Any player who has that number covers it with a red square. Put all the blue squares back in the 🛍. Repeat until one player wins.

Cover Nine

5	4	2
6	2	5
1	6	3

Cover Nine

3	4	1
6	2	3
4	1	5

To win, be the first player to cover nine game spaces.

Try Again Play again!

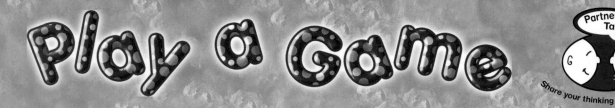

Play a Game

Partner Talk

Share your thinking while you work.

Start  Count 8 blue squares with your partner. Put them in a 🛍. Get 18 red squares. Give one game board to each player. Play at the same time.

Try Take some squares from the 🛍. Count them. How many squares are still in the 🛍? Check your answer by counting. Look on your game board for the word that names the number of squares that were left in the 🛍. Any player who has that word covers it with a red square. Put all the blue squares back in the 🛍. Repeat until one player wins.

Cover Nine

one	five	four
three	two	six
one	four	three

Cover Nine

six	one	five
two	three	one
five	four	two

To win, be the first player to cover nine game spaces.

Try Again Play again!

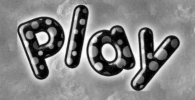 **Play a Game**

 Partner Talk — *Share your thinking while you work.*

 **Start** 👫 Put ①②③④⑤⑥⑦⑧ in a 🛍.

Get 20 red squares.
Give one game board to each player. Play at the same time.

Try Pick a tile. Put it in the space above PART I KNOW. Talk about ways to find the MISSING PART of 9. Any player who has the MISSING PART of 9 can cover that number with a red square.
Put the tile back in the 🛍.
Repeat until one player wins.

Player 1	
8	6
4	5
3	6
7	1
2	4

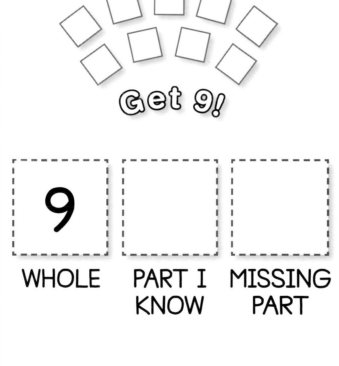

Get 9!

9		
WHOLE	PART I KNOW	MISSING PART

To win, be the first player to cover 9 game spaces.

Player 2	
7	4
5	2
8	1
3	6
2	5

Try Again Play again!

Play a Game

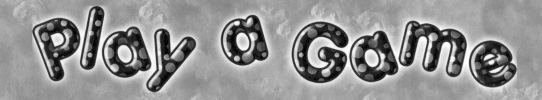

Start 👫 Put  in a .

Get 20 red squares.
Give one game board to each player. Play at the same time.

Try Pick a tile. Put it in the PART I KNOW square. Talk about ways to find the MISSING PART of 9. Look at your game board. Do you see a way to show the MISSING PART? If yes, cover that game space with a red square. Put the tile back in the 🛍.
Repeat until one player wins.

Get 9!

Player 1

3 + 3	1 + 1
1 + 3	1 + 0
2 + 4	1 + 2
4 + 1	5 + 2
2 + 2	4 + 4

9		
WHOLE	PART I KNOW	MISSING PART

Player 2

1 + 1	3 + 4
3 + 3	2 + 0
0 + 1	4 + 4
4 + 1	2 + 1
2 + 2	0 + 5

To win, be the first player to cover 9 game spaces.

Try Again Play again!

Partner Talk

Share your thinking while you work.

Start Get a 🎲.
Get 5 red squares for one player.
Get 5 blue squares for the other player.
Take turns.

Try Toss the 🎲. Place it in the space below.
Subtract that number from 7. Say the difference.
If you see the number sentence on the game board, cover it with a square.
Repeat until one player wins.

$$7 - \boxed{\text{Put cube here}} = ?$$

Win with Five

7 - 1 = 6	7 - 6 = 1	7 - 4 = 3
7 - 4 = 3	7 - 1 = 6	7 - 5 = 2
7 - 2 = 5	7 - 3 = 4	7 - 2 = 5

To win, be the first player who covers 5 game spaces.

Try Again Play again!

Play a Game

Start 👫 Put  in a 🛍️ .

Get a 🎲 .
Get 5 red squares for one player.
Get 5 blue squares for the other player. Take turns.

Try Pick a tile. Toss the 🎲 . Place them in the two spaces below.
Subtract the number on the 🎲 from the number on the tile.
Say the subtraction sentence. If you see the difference on the game board, cover it with a square.

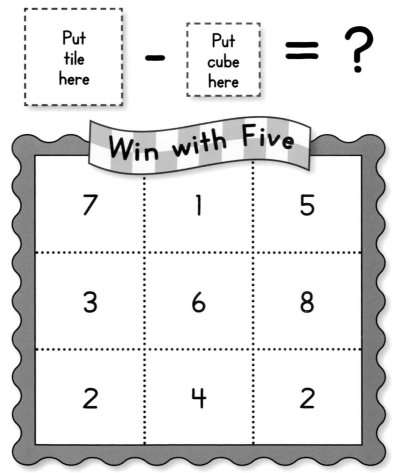

| Put tile here | − | Put cube here | = ? |

Win with Five

7	1	5
3	6	8
2	4	2

To win, be the first player who covers 5 game spaces.

Try Again Play again!

Helping Hands

Partner Talk

Share your thinking while you work.

Start 👫 Get a 🎲.
Get 9 blue squares.
Take turns until each player has 3 turns.

Try Toss the 🎲. Find your toss below.
Follow the directions.
Put squares in the rectangle at the bottom of the page.
Ask your partner to watch.
Ask your partner to say a subtraction sentence to show what you did.

⚀	Put 7 squares in the rectangle. Move 3 below the rectangle.
⚁	Put 8 squares in the rectangle. Move 1 below the rectangle.
⚂	Put 9 squares in the rectangle. Move 5 below the rectangle.

⚃	Put 6 squares in the rectangle. Move 2 below the rectangle.
⚄	Put 7 squares in the rectangle. Move 4 below the rectangle.
⚅	Put 8 squares in the rectangle. Move 2 below the rectangle.

Try Again Use squares to make your own story about taking away.
Talk about how you find the difference.

Center Activity ⭐ **2-5**

Helping Hands

Partner Talk

Share your thinking while you work.

Start 👫 Get a 🎲.
Get 9 blue squares.
Take turns until each player has 3 turns.

Try Toss the 🎲. Find your toss below.
Follow the directions.
Read the subtraction sentence.
Use squares to show what it means.
Put all the squares in the circle.
Move some squares
outside the circle.

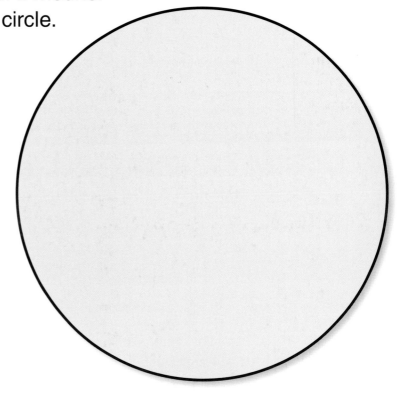

🎲	9 - 6 = 3
🎲	7 - 2 = 5
🎲	8 - 2 = 6
🎲	9 - 7 = 2
🎲	7 - 4 = 3
🎲	9 - 5 = 4

Try Again Use squares to act out a story about taking away.
Ask your partner to say a subtraction sentence for your story.

Partner Talk
Share your thinking while you work.

Try Together

 **Start** Put 7 8 9 in a  .

Get a 🎲 . Get 9 red squares. Get 6 blue squares.
Work together.

Try

Pick a tile.
Cover that number
of these pots with
red squares.

Toss the cube.
Cover that number
of these pots with
blue squares.

Say a subtraction sentence to show how many more
red pots than blue pots you will use.

Try Again Repeat several times.
Talk about subtracting to compare.
What does the difference mean?

Try Together

Partner Talk

Share your thinking while you work.

Start 🚶 Get one ⤿. Get 9 red squares.
Get 6 blue squares. Work together.

Try Put a ⤿ next to a subtraction sentence.
Read the subtraction sentence.

9 - 2 = 7	9 - 5 = 4	9 - 3 = 6
6 - 5 = 1	6 - 4 = 2	9 - 5 = 4
8 - 3 = 5	7 - 3 = 4	8 - 6 = 2
8 - 2 = 6	7 - 2 = 5	7 - 4 = 3

Cover the pots below to show the subtraction sentence.
Explain what the difference means.

Put red squares on these pots
to show the first number.

Put blue squares on these pots
to show the second number.

Try Again Make your own subtraction sentence.
Explain how you can use it to compare.

Listen and Learn

Partner Talk

Share your thinking while you work.

Start 👫 Get 8 blue squares. Use them to cover the game spaces on the Left Chart. Get 13 red squares.

Get ⬜1 ⬜2 ⬜3 ⬜4 ⬜5 ⬜6 ⬜7 ⬜8 . Take turns.

Try Uncover a game space on the Left Chart. Say the number sentence. Use red squares and the part-part-whole mat to find the answer. Cover the missing part on the Right Chart with a number tile.

8 – 3 = ☐	7 – 0 = ☐	10 – 4 = ☐
3 – 1 = ☐	**Left Chart**	8 – 7 = ☐
11 – 7 = ☐	13 – 5 = ☐	10 – 7 = ☐

1	2	3
4	**Right Chart**	5
6	7	8

Play until all of the game spaces are uncovered.

Whole	
Part	Part

Try Again Play again! Talk about how you find the missing part.

Listen and Learn

Start 👫 Get 18 red squares.
Get one ⬭ and one ✏️ to make a spinner.
Take turns.

Try Spin on the Number Sentence Wheel. Say the number sentence. Then spin on the Picture Wheel. Make up a story using the number sentence and the picture. Tell the story to your partner as you solve it on the part-part-whole mat.

Number Sentence Wheel

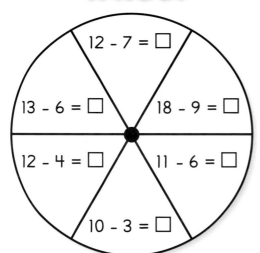

Picture Wheel

Play until each player gets 4 turns.

Whole	
Part	Part

Try Again This time, choose the number sentence and the picture you like.

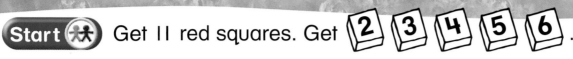 # Helping Hands

Partner Talk

Share your thinking while you work.

Start  Get 11 red squares. Get ②③④⑤⑥.

Try Pick and read a story problem together. Use red squares on the part-part-whole mat to solve. Say a number sentence that matches the story. Then use a number tile to answer the question.

Al put 7 on the table. Later there was 1 left. How many were eaten?

Tammy planted 3 . Now her garden has 8 . How many  were already in the garden?

Mike has 4 . He has 7 . How many more than does Mike have?

Cam needs 6 to make . He has 4 . How many more does Cam need?

Whole	
Part	Part

Try Again This time, make up a subtraction story for your partner to solve.

Helping Hands

Partner Talk

Share your thinking while you work.

Start 👥 Get 8 red squares. Get one ⊂⊃.
Work together.

Try Pick a story problem. Use red squares on the part-part-whole mat to solve it. Say the answer. Then put a ⊂⊃ on the type of problem you solved.

Ian has 8 ⚾. Reyna gives him 3 more ⚾. How many ⚾ does Ian have now?

Jacob has 5 ✏. He gave away some. Now he has 2 ✏. How many did he give away?

Carl's 📦 holds 6 📖. He puts in 3 📖. How many more 📖 will fit in the 📦?

Maya has 7 💍. Some are pink and some are green. 3 💍 are pink. How many are green?

Types of Problems to Solve

Taking Away	Joining	Missing Part	Comparing

Whole	
Part	Part

Try Again This time, make up a math story for your partner. Talk about different kinds of subtraction problems.

Helping Hands

Partner Talk

Share your thinking while you work.

Start 👥 Get  3 4 5 6 7 .

Get a 🎲 . Get 7 red squares. Work together.

Try Toss the 🎲 . Use red squares to show the parts.
Use a tile to show the whole. Follow the directions.

⚀	Put 2 squares in one part. Put 3 squares in the other part.
⚀	Put 1 square in one part. Put 3 squares in the other part.
⚂	Put 2 squares in one part. Put 4 squares in the other part.

⚁	Put 1 square in one part. Put 2 squares in the other part.
⚄	Put 4 squares in one part. Put 3 squares in the other part.
⚅	Put 5 squares in one part. Put 2 squares in the other part.

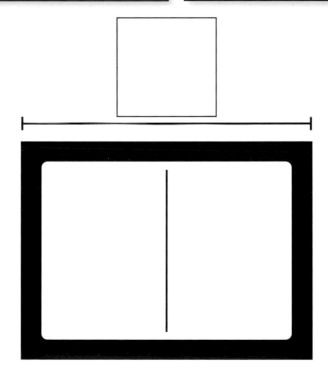

After you display the squares, say one addition sentence
and two subtraction sentences with those numbers.

Try Again Repeat the activity.

Helping Hands

Partner Talk
Share your thinking while you work.

Start 🏃 Get 6 7 8 9.

Get a 🎲. Get 9 red squares. Work together.

Try Toss the 🎲. Use red squares to show the parts.
Use a tile to show the whole. Follow the directions.

⚀	Put 4 squares in one part. Put 5 squares in the other part.
⚁	Put 3 squares in one part. Put 4 squares in the other part.
⚂	Put 3 squares in one part. Put 5 squares in the other part.

⚂	Put 8 squares in one part. Put 1 square in the other part.
⚄	Put 2 squares in one part. Put 4 squares in the other part.
⚅	Put 6 squares in one part. Put 3 squares in the other part.

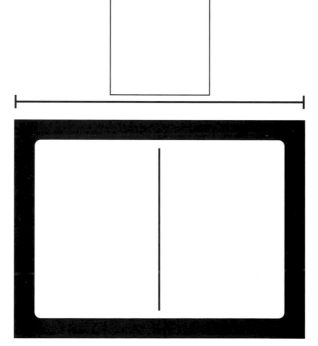

After you display the squares, say two addition sentences
and two subtraction sentences with those numbers.

Try Again Repeat the activity. Talk about the number sentences you could
say if you had the same number of squares in each part.

Play a Game

Partner Talk
Share your thinking while you work.

 **Start** Put ⟨7⟩ ⟨8⟩ ⟨9⟩ in a 🛍️.

Get 2 🎲.
Get 5 red squares for one player.
Get 5 blue squares for the other player. Take turns.

Try Pick a tile. Toss the 🎲. Make the subtraction sentences below.
Subtract the number on the 🎲 from the number on the tile.
Say the subtraction sentences. If you see the difference on the
game board, cover it with a square.

| Put tile here | − | Put cube here | = ? | ? = | Put tile here | − | Put cube here |

Win with Five

7	1	5
3	6	8
2	4	2

To win, be the first player who covers 5 game spaces.

Try Again Play again!

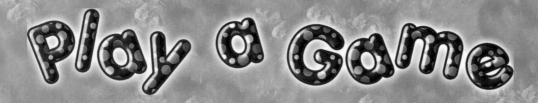

Partner Talk

Share your thinking while you work.

Start 👫 Get a 🎲.
Get 5 red squares for one player.
Get 5 blue squares for the other player.
Take turns.

Try Toss the 🎲. Place it in the space below.
Subtract that number from 8. Say the difference.
If you see the number sentence in a different order on the game board,
cover it with a square. Repeat until one player wins.

$$8 - \boxed{\text{Put cube here}} = ?$$

Win with Five

6 = 8 - 2	7 = 8 - 1	4 = 8 - 4
3 = 8 - 5	2 = 8 - 6	3 = 8 - 5
5 = 8 - 3	7 = 8 - 1	6 = 8 - 2

To win, be the first player who covers 5 game spaces.

Try Again Play again!

Listen and Learn

Partner Talk

Share your thinking while you work.

Start 👤 Get  1 2 3 4 5 6 7 8 9 .

Get a 🎲. Take turns until each player gets 5 turns.

Try Toss the 🎲. Find the number you tossed below. Tell your partner a subtraction story about that picture. Ask your partner to use the numbers in your story to show a number sentence with tiles. Say that number sentence. Explain why it matches your story.

🎲 (1)	butterflies	_____ − _____ = _____
🎲 (2)	ants	_____ − _____ = _____
🎲 (3)	birds	_____ − _____ = _____
🎲 (4)	ladybugs	_____ − _____ = _____
🎲 (5)	dragonflies	_____ − _____ = _____
🎲 (6)	caterpillars	_____ − _____ = _____

Try Again Make up a subtraction story. Ask your partner to say a number sentence with the numbers in your story.

Listen and Learn

Partner Talk

Share your thinking while you work.

Start 👥 Put 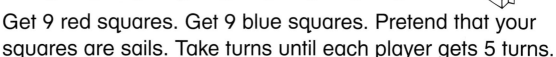 in a 🛍.

Get 9 red squares. Get 9 blue squares. Pretend that your squares are sails. Take turns until each player gets 5 turns.

Try Pick a tile. Put red sails on that number of boats. Ask your partner to put blue sails on the other boats. How many boats would be left if the boats with red sails sailed away? Say a subtraction sentence with the numbers in your story. Put the tile back in the 🛍.

Try Again Say a subtraction sentence. Begin with 9 in all. Ask your partner to tell a story about the boats to match your subtraction sentence.

Try Together

Partner Talk

Share your thinking while you work.

Start 👥 Put  in a .

Get 10 red squares. Take turns.

Try Pick a tile. Use squares to show that number on the ten-frame.
Point to a flower that tells about the number.
Read the sentence to your partner.

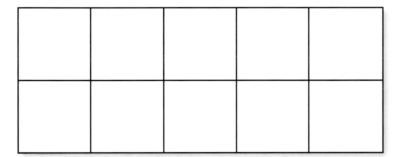

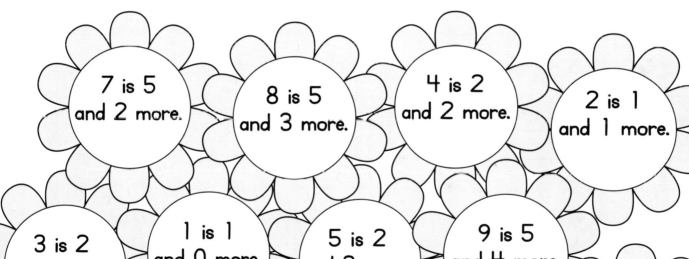

7 is 5 and 2 more.

8 is 5 and 3 more.

4 is 2 and 2 more.

2 is 1 and 1 more.

3 is 2 and 1 more.

1 is 1 and 0 more.

5 is 2 and 3 more.

9 is 5 and 4 more.

6 is 5 and 1 more.

Try Again Talk about how you would describe 10 on the ten-frame.

Center Activity ★ **3-1**

Try Together

Start 👥 Get 10 red squares. Take turns.

Try Point to a tea cup.
Tell your partner what that number looks like on the ten-frame.
Use squares to show that number on the ten-frame.
Ask your partner to find the teapot that matches.

Try Again Point to a teapot. Say the sentence. Ask your partner to put squares on the ten-frame to match what you say.

Cover Three

Start 👫 Get a 🎲 . Get 6 red squares.
Get 6 blue squares. Take turns.

Try Toss the 🎲 . Say the number.
Point to it on a ten-frame.
Do you see a sentence about your
number on the game board?

If you do, say it to your partner.
Then cover it with a square.

If not, lose your turn.

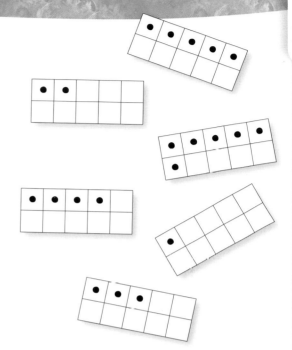

My number is 4 away from 5.	My number fills a whole row.	My number is 1 away from 5.
My number is 2 away from 5.	My number is 5 and 1 more.	My number is 4 away from 5.
My number is 5 and 1 more.	My number is 3 away from 5.	My number fills a whole row.

To win, get: ■■■ or ■ or ■ or ■

Try Again Play again!

Cover Three

Start 🧑 Put  in a .

Get 6 red squares. Get 6 blue squares. Take turns.

Try Pick a tile. Tell how that number looks on a ten-frame.
Find a sentence about your number on the game board.
Say it to your partner. Then, cover it with a square.
Set the tile aside.

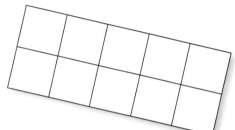

My number is 2 away from 5.	My number is 5 and 1 more.	My number fills up a whole row.
My number is 3 away from 5.	My number is 9 away from 10.	My number is 5 and 3 more.
My number is 1 away from 5.	My number is 5 and 2 more.	My number is 1 away from 2 full rows.

To win, get: ■■■ or ▪ or ■   or   ■
                      ■   ■
                      ■   ■   ■

Try Again Play again!

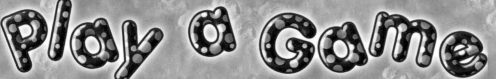

Play a Game

Partner Talk

Share your thinking while you work.

Start 🧍 Get a 🎲. Get 20 red squares.
Give one game board to each player.
Take turns.

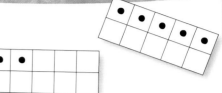

Try Toss the 🎲. Point to that number on a ten-frame.
How many more dots do you need to make 10?
Cover that number on your game board.
If you do not see that number, lose your turn.

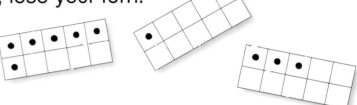

Player 1		MAKE 10!	Player 2	
5	4		8	7
9	6		5	9
7	8	To win, be the first player to cover 10 game spaces.	7	5
4	9		4	6
8	5		9	8

Try Again Play again!

Play a Game

Partner Talk

Share your thinking while you work.

Start 🖐 Put ⬚1 ⬚2 ⬚3 ⬚4 ⬚6 ⬚7 ⬚8 ⬚9 in a 🛍.

Get 20 red squares.
Give one game board to each player. Take turns.

Try Pick two tiles. Put them here. ⟶ ☐ and ☐
If you have two parts of 10, use your
finger to trace around those two parts
of 10 on the ten-frame. Cover those
two parts of 10 on your game board.
If you do not have two parts of 10, lose your turn.
Put the tiles back in the 🛍.

Player 1 · MAKE 10! · Player 2

Player 1		MAKE 10!	Player 2	
9 and 1	4 and 6	• • • • • / • • • • •	7 and 3	1 and 9
3 and 7	2 and 8		4 and 6	2 and 8
6 and 4	1 and 9	To win, be the first player to cover two game spaces.	9 and 1	4 and 6
8 and 2	7 and 3		8 and 2	3 and 7
4 and 6	9 and 1		6 and 4	9 and 1

Try Again Play again!

Look and See

Partner Talk

Share your thinking while you work.

Start 🚶 Get a 🎲. Get 9 red squares. Get 9 blue squares.
Take turns until each partner gets 5 or more turns.

Try Toss the 🎲. Say the number.
That is the number of marbles in the bag.
Use red squares to show that number on the ten-frame.
Ask your partner to show how many more
marbles you need to get ten in the bag.
Let your partner show the answer with
blue squares on the ten-frame.
Point to the marbles that will be
added to the bag.

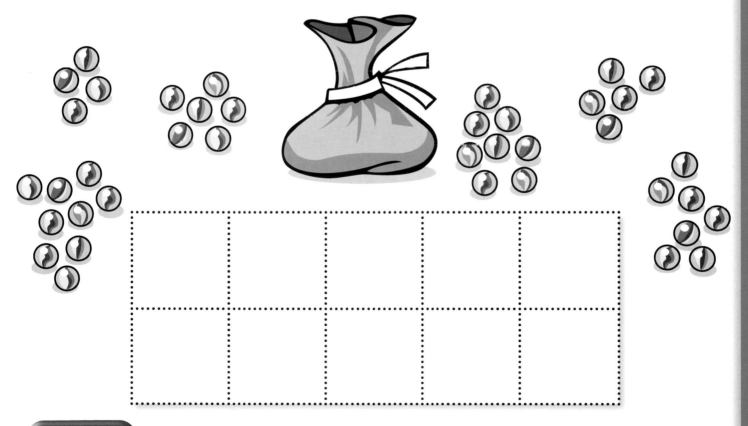

Try Again Talk about how a ten-frame helps us
to find a missing part of 10.

Center Activity ★ 3-4

Look and See

Start  Put 1 2 3 4 5 6 7 8 9 in a 🛍️.

Get 9 red squares.
Take turns until the 🛍️ is empty.

Try Pick a tile. Put it on the basket. That is the number of apples in the basket. Find a plate that shows some apples that can be added to the basket to make 10 in all.
Use the ten-frame to help you. Use a square to cover that plate.
Set the tile aside.

Try Again Remove the squares. Point to a plate. Ask your partner to tell you how many more apples you need to make 10.

Partner Talk

Share your thinking while you work.

Start  Put   0 1 2 3 4 5 6 7 8 9 in a .

Give one table to each player. Play the game 3 times.

	Player 1		Player 2	
Try Pick a tile. The player who needs that tile to make 10 in one row of a table takes the tile and puts it in that row. Keep picking and placing tiles until one table is completed. The first player who completes a table wins.	📖	🧸	🚲	📖
		9	6	
	2			3
		7	8	
	4			1
		5	10	

Try Again Pretend you are going on a trip.
You want to take some toys and books.
You want 10 things in all. How many of each would you take?

Play a Game

Partner Talk

Share your thinking while you work.

Start 👤 Put  1 2 3 4 5 6 7 8 9 in a 🛍.

Get 0 1 2 3 4 5 6 7 8 9.

Give one table to each player. Play the game 3 times.

	Player 1		Player 2	
Try Take turns. Pick a tile from the 🛍. Place it in a shaded space in your table. When the bag is empty, put the 0–9 tiles in the 🛍. Pick a tile. If you need it to make 10 in all in one row of your table, put it in your table. If not, put the tile back in the 🛍. The first player who completes a table wins.	📖	🧸	🚲	📖
			10	

Try Again Pretend you are going on a trip.
You want to take some toys and books.
You want 10 things in all. How many of each could you take?

Play a Game

Start  Put ⬚0⬚ ⬚1⬚ ⬚2⬚ in a .

Get 18 red squares. Give one game board to each player.
Take turns.

Try Pick a number above the game board.
Then take a tile from the 🛍. Explain how to add those
two numbers. Cover the sum if you see it on the game board.
Put the tile back in the 🛍.

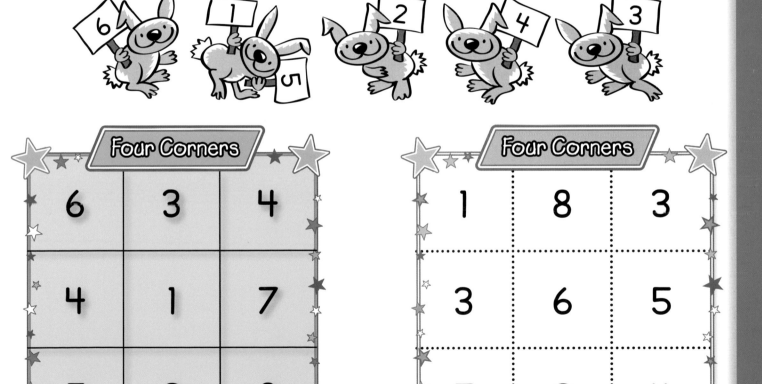

To win, be the first player who covers four corners.

Try Again Play again!

Start 🏃 Put 0 1 2 in a 🛍.

Get 18 red squares. Give one game board to each player.
Take turns.

Try Pick a number above the game board.
Then take a tile from the 🛍. Explain how to add those
two numbers. Cover the sum if you see it on your game board.
Put the tile back in the 🛍.

10 15 11 16 13 8
7 3 9 12

Four Corners		
15	4	9
8	17	13
12	5	11

Four Corners		
7	12	14
15	10	13
16	3	18

To win, be the first player who covers four corners.

Try Again Play again!

Math in Motion

Partner Talk — Share your thinking while you work.

Start 👤 or 👥 Put ⬜1 ⬜2 ⬜3 ⬜4 ⬜5 ⬜6 in a 🛍️.

Work alone, or take turns.

Try Pick a tile.

Show the number. Tap on this drum.

Show the same number. Tap on this drum.

Say the doubles fact.
For example, *3 plus 3 equals 6.*

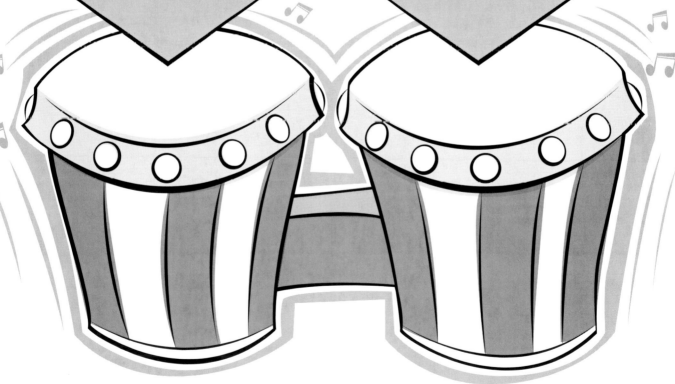

Try Again Repeat until the 🛍️ of tiles is empty.
Put the tiles back in the 🛍️. Practice again!

Math in Motion

Start 👥 Decide who will go first.

Try ➡️ Point to a number that is the sum for a doubles fact.

1	2	3	4
5	6	7	8
9	10	11	12

Ask your partner to say the doubles for that number.
Make the same number of taps on each drum.

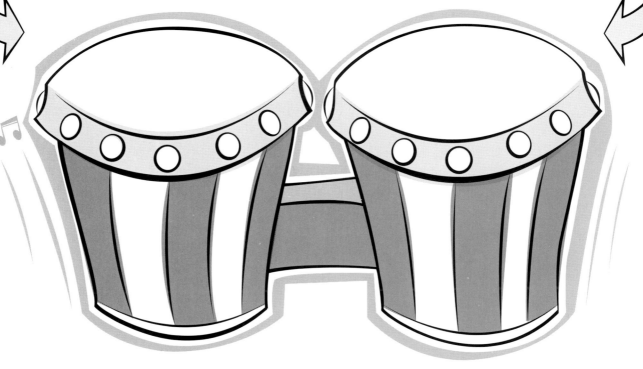

Try Again Use every possible number in the chart.
Point to all of the numbers you used.
Look for a pattern. Explain the pattern to your partner.

Try Together

Start 👫 Get 5 red squares for Player 1.
Get 5 blue squares for Player 2. Take turns.

Try Point to a double around the necklace. Ask your partner to point to its near double. Tell why using that double is helpful for adding its near double. Put squares on both addition facts.

Say: The double _____ + _____ = _____

helps me find the near double

_____ + _____ = _____

because. . .

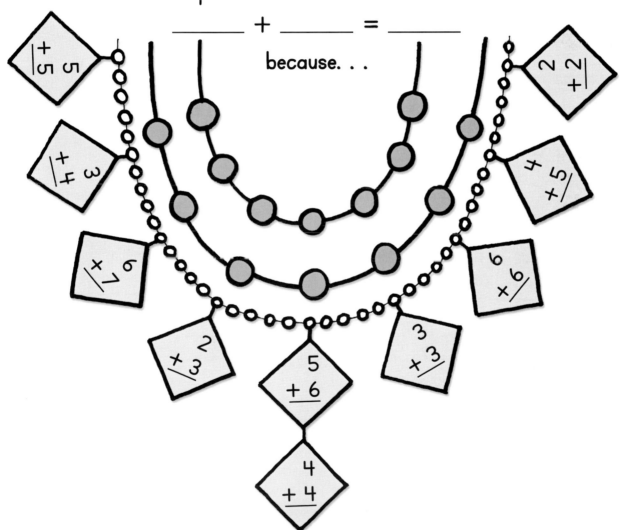

Try Again Talk about how the beads can help you to add a double and a near double.

Try Together

Partner Talk

Share your thinking while you work.

Start  Put 1 2 3 4 5 6 7 8 in a 🛍️.

Get 4 red squares for Player 1.
Get 4 blue squares for Player 2. Take turns.

Try Pick a tile. Double that number.
Ask your partner to find and say its near double.
Put a square on its near double.

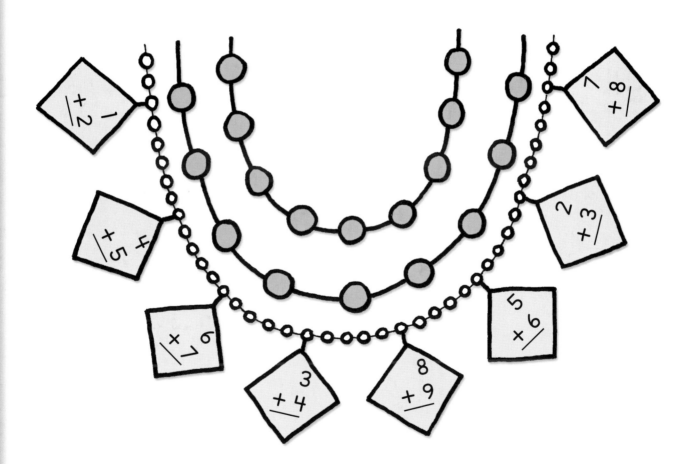

Try Again Talk about why we double the lesser addend
and then add 1 to solve a near double.

Start Put 0 1 2 3 4 in a .

Get 6 red squares. Get 6 blue squares. Take turns.

Try Pick one tile. Add that number to 5. Point to the ten-frame that shows the sum. How many more do you need to get 10? If you see the answer to that question on the game board, cover that space. Put the tiles back in the .

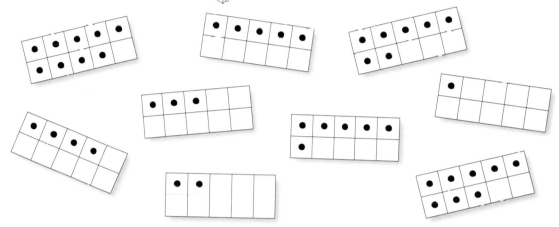

6 + 4 = 10	8 + 2 = 10	7 + 3 = 10
8 + 2 = 10	7 + 3 = 10	9 + 1 = 10
9 + 1 = 10	6 + 4 = 10	5 + 5 = 10

To win, get:

Try Again Play again!

Center Activity ★ 4-4

Cover Three

Partner Talk
Share your thinking while you work.

Start  Put 1 2 3 4 5 6 7 8 9 in a 🛍.

Get 6 red squares. Get 6 blue squares.
Take turns until the 🛍 is empty.

Try Pick one tile and say that number.
Read the sentence that begins with that number.
If you see a ten-frame that matches what you said, cover it.

| 1 and 9 more is 10. | 5 and 5 more is 10. | 6 and 4 more is 10. |

| 4 and 6 more is 10. | 2 and 8 more is 10. | 7 and 3 more is 10. |

| 3 and 7 more is 10. | 8 and 2 more is 10. | 9 and 1 more is 10. |

To win, get: ■ ■ ■ or ■ or ■ or ■
■ ■ ■
■ ■ ■

Try Again Play again!

Helping Hands

Start 👫 Get a 🎲. Get 9 red squares. Get 9 blue squares.
Work together.

Try Toss the 🎲. Follow the directions. Fill the top ten-frame
with red squares. Fill the bottom ten-frame with blue squares.
Now show how you can make a ten to add those two numbers.

🎲	Use 7 red and 4 blue squares.	🎲	Use 8 red and 4 blue squares.
🎲	Use 8 red and 3 blue squares.	🎲	Use 7 red and 5 blue squares.
🎲	Use 9 red and 2 blue squares.	🎲	Use 9 red and 3 blue squares.

10 + 1

10 + 2

Try Again Point to one of the rectangles around the ten-frames.
Say the sum for those numbers.
Find two other numbers that have the same sum.

Helping Hands

Partner Talk

Share your thinking while you work.

Start 👫 Get 9 red squares. Work together.

Try Choose a puddle. Say the sum for those two addends.
Look at each umbrella. Point to an umbrella that has
the same sum as the puddle. Use the raindrops to explain why.
Cover the umbrella under those raindrops.
Repeat until every umbrella is covered.

10 + 1

10 + 5

10 + 4

10 + 7

10 + 2

10 + 3

10 + 6

8 + 5   9 + 7   5 + 6   6 + 8

7 + 8   5 + 7   9 + 8   8 + 7   9 + 4

Try Again Remove the squares. Point to two addends in an umbrella.
Ask your partner to point to a puddle that has the same sum.

Play a Game

Partner Talk
Share your thinking while you work.

Start  Put 0 1 2 in a 🛍.

Get 18 red squares.
Give one game board to each player. Take turns.

Try Point to a number on the activity mat. Pick a tile from the 🛍.

Say: "☐ less than ⭐ is _____ ."

If that answer is on your game board, cover it. Put the tile back in the 🛍. Repeat until one player wins.

Activity Mat

9   6   4
3   2   7
5   10   8

Cover Nine

8	2	0
4	9	7
1	5	3

Cover Nine

6	1	5
3	8	0
2	9	7

To win, be the first player to cover nine game spaces.

Try Again Play again!

Play a Game

Partner Talk
Share your thinking while you work.

Start 🏃 Put **0** **1** **2** **3** **4** **5** **6** **7** **8** **9** in a .

Get 18 red squares. Give one game board to each player.
Play at the same time.

Try Pick a tile. Put it in the square on the activity mat.

Say: "My number is 2 less than _____ ."

If that answer is on your game board, cover it.
Put the tile aside. Repeat until one person wins.

Activity Mat

| My number | is 2 less than _____ . |

Cover Nine

2	8	5
9	4	7
6	10	11

Cover Nine

2	7	5
10	8	9
4	11	3

To win, be the first player to cover nine game spaces.

Try Again Play again!

Helping Hands

Partner Talk — Share your thinking while you work.

Start 👥 Put  1 2 3 4 5 in a 🛍 . Take turns.

Try Pick a tile. Show that number with your fingers. Have your partner show the same number of fingers. Say the addition fact for your double. Ask your partner to look below and read the related subtraction fact. Set the tile aside. Repeat until the 🛍 is empty.

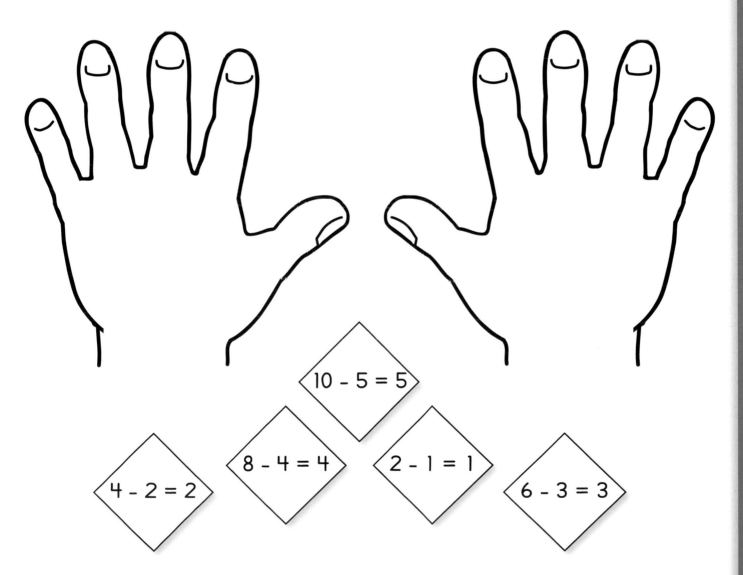

$$10 - 5 = 5$$

$$8 - 4 = 4 \qquad 2 - 1 = 1$$

$$4 - 2 = 2 \qquad\qquad 6 - 3 = 3$$

Try Again Put the tiles back in the 🛍 . Repeat the activity.

Helping Hands

Partner Talk

Share your thinking while you work.

Start 👥 Put ⟨1⟩ ⟨2⟩ ⟨3⟩ ⟨4⟩ ⟨5⟩ in a 🛍. Take turns.

Try Pick a tile. Show that number with your fingers.
Have your partner show the same number of fingers.
Say the addition fact for your double. Ask your partner
to say a related subtraction fact. Set the tile aside.
Repeat until the 🛍 is empty.

Try Again Put the tiles back in the 🛍. Repeat the activity.
Talk about how knowing addition facts for doubles
can help you learn subtraction facts.

Center Activity ★ ★ 4-7

Try Together

Start 👥 Put  in a 🛍️.

Look at the flowers.
Every flower had 8 petals.
Some petals fell off. Take turns.
For each flower, say an addition fact.
Say the number of petals you see on the flower, and
the number that are missing. Make sure you get 8 in all.

Try Take turns again. Pick a tile.
Put the tile on a flower with that number of petals.
Say a subtraction sentence that begins with 8 in all.
Put the tile aside. Repeat until the 🛍️ is empty.

Try Again Put the tiles back in the 🛍️. Repeat the activity.
Talk about how addition and subtraction are related.

Try Together

Partner Talk

Share your thinking while you work.

Start 😊 Get a ✏️ .

Put  **0 1 2 3 4 5 6 7 8** in a 🛍️ .

Work together.

Try Pick a tile. Put that number of tulips in one group.
To make two groups, gently lay your ✏️ on the page.

Say an addition fact with your
two parts and 8 in all.
Then say a related subtraction fact.

Put the tile aside. Repeat until the 🛍️ is empty.

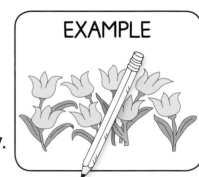

EXAMPLE

Try Again Put the tiles back in the 🛍️. Repeat the activity. This time,
try to say two addition facts and two related subtraction facts.
Can you do this for every number in the 🛍️?

Look and See

Partner Talk
Share your thinking while you work.

Start 👥 Put 4 4 5 5 6 6 in a 🛍️.

Get 12 red squares. Work together.

Try Pick a tile. Put that number of red squares on the left wing.
Pick another tile. Put that number of red squares on the right wing.
Say an addition fact that has your two parts.
Say a subtraction fact that has your two parts.

Try Again Remove the squares. Put the tiles back in the 🛍️.
Repeat the activity several times. What do you find out
by adding? What do you find out by subtracting?

Center Activity ★ 4-9

Look and See

Partner Talk

Share your thinking while you work.

Start Put **3 4 5 6 7 8 9** in a 🛍️.

Get 12 red squares. Work together.

Try Decide if you want the butterfly to have 9, 10, 11, or 12 spots in all.
Pick a tile. Put that number of squares on the left wing.
How many squares will you put on the right wing?

Say: _____ – _____ = _____

Spots in all — Spots on the left wing — Spots on the right wing

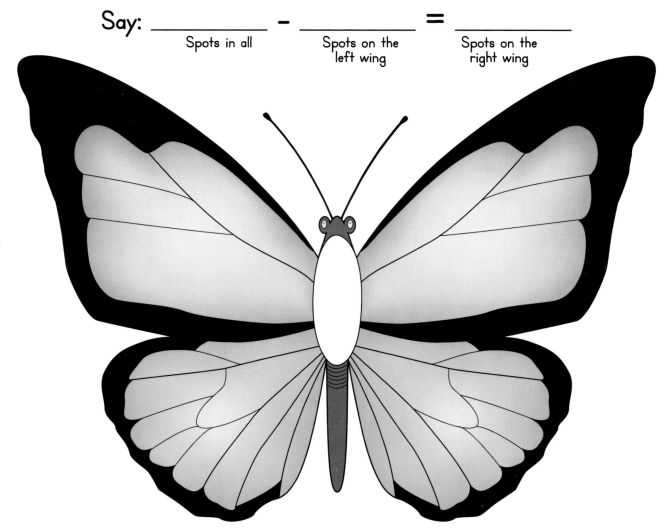

Try Again Remove the squares. Put the tiles back in the 🛍️.
Repeat several times. How can you use an addition fact
to help you subtract?

Look and See

Partner Talk

Share your thinking while you work.

Start 👥 Put 1 2 3 4 5 6 7 8 9 in a .

Get 9 red squares. Pretend your squares are fish. Take turns.

Try Pick a tile. Put that number of fish in the ocean to swim with these fish. How many fish are there in all?

Put your tile in the number sentence.
Ask your partner to say the complete number sentence.
Put the tile back in the 🛍.

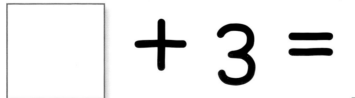

☐ + 3 = ____

Try Again This time, place a number tile in the number sentence.
Ask your partner to make a picture with fish.
Say the complete number sentence.

Look and See

Start 👫 Put [1] [2] [3] [4] [5] [6] [7] [8] [9] in a .

Get 9 red squares. Get 9 blue squares.
Pretend your squares are fish. Take turns.

Try Pick a tile. Show that number of red fish in the ocean. Pick another tile. Show that number of blue fish in the ocean. How many fish are swimming in the ocean?

Put your tiles in the number sentence.
Ask your partner to say the complete number sentence.
Put the tiles back in the 🛍.

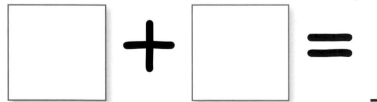

Try Again This time, place number tiles in the number sentence.
Ask your partner to make a picture with fish.
Say the complete number sentence.

Look and See

Start  Put 0 2 4 6 7 8 in a .

Give one game board to each player.
Get 6 squares for each player. Take turns.

Try Pick a tile. Point to the animals next to that number.
Say a doubles fact to match their legs.
Cover the fact if you see it on your game board.
Put the tile back in the 📄.

Player 1

7 + 7 = 14	6 + 6 = 12	2 + 2 = 4
0 + 0 = 0	4 + 4 = 8	8 + 8 = 16

Player 2

4 + 4 = 8	0 + 0 = 0	8 + 8 = 16
6 + 6 = 12	7 + 7 = 14	2 + 2 = 4

To win, be the first to cover four game spaces.

Try Again Say four doubles facts that are not on your game board.

Center Activity ★ 5-1

Look and See

Partner Talk

Share your thinking while you work.

Start  Put ⬜0 ⬜2 ⬜4 ⬜6 ⬜7 ⬜8 in a 🛍️.

Give one game board to each player.
Get 6 squares for each player. Take turns.

Try Pick a tile. Point to the animals next to that number.
How many legs would two of those animals have?
Cover the sum if you see it on your game board.
Put the tile back in the 🛍️.

Player 1

14 in all	12 in all	4 in all
0 in all	8 in all	16 in all

Player 2

8 in all	0 in all	16 in all
12 in all	14 in all	4 in all

To win, be the first to cover four game spaces.

Try Again Say a doubles fact for every number on your game board.
Then tell other doubles facts that you know.

Helping Hands

Partner Talk
Share your thinking while you work.

Start Put 1 2 3 4 5 6 7 8 in a .

Get 17 squares. Take turns.

Try Pick a tile. Put that number of squares in the left column. Ask your partner to put the same number of squares in the right column.
Say the doubles fact.

Add an extra square. Point to and say the doubles-plus-1 fact. Remove the squares. Repeat until the 🛍 is empty.

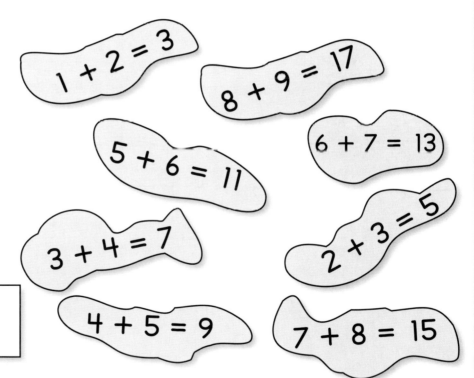

$1 + 2 = 3$

$8 + 9 = 17$

$5 + 6 = 11$

$6 + 7 = 13$

$3 + 4 = 7$

$2 + 3 = 5$

$4 + 5 = 9$

$7 + 8 = 15$

_____ + _____ and 1 more

Try Again Point to a doubles-plus-1 fact.
Ask your partner to show that fact with squares.

Helping Hands

Partner Talk

Share your thinking while you work.

Start 👥 Get 8 squares. Cover all the numbers on the right with the squares. Take turns.

Try Uncover a number. Which picture has that number of dots in all? Point to it. Say the doubles-plus-1 fact for those dots.

Use your square to cover the doubles-plus-1 fact on the left. Repeat until every number in the right column is uncovered.

6 + 7
2 + 3
7 + 8
1 + 2
4 + 5
8 + 9
3 + 4
5 + 6

11
13
3
5
9
15
17
7

Try Again This time, cover all the facts on the left. Then play the opposite way.

Helping Hands

Partner Talk
Share your thinking while you work.

Start  Put   in a .

Get 20 squares. Take turns.

Try Pick a tile. Put that number of squares in the left column. Ask your partner to put the same number of squares in the right column. Say the doubles fact.

Add two extra squares. Point to and say the doubles-plus-2 fact. Repeat until the is empty.

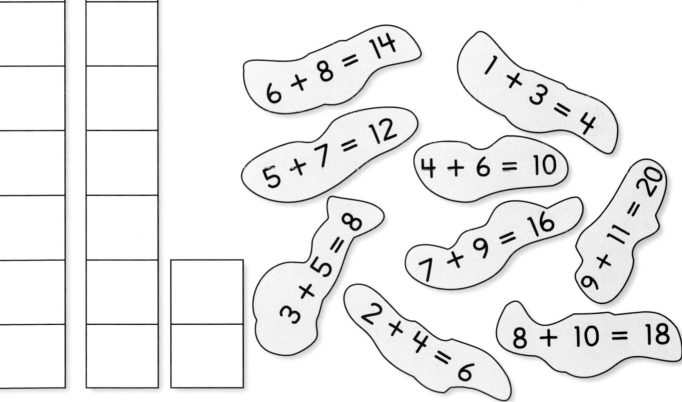

_____ + _____ and 2 more

Try Again Point to a doubles-plus-2 fact.
Ask your partner to show that fact with squares.

Helping Hands

Start 👫 Get 8 squares. Cover all the numbers on the right with the squares. Take turns.

6 + 8
2 + 4
7 + 9
1 + 3
4 + 6
8 + 10
3 + 5
5 + 7

Try Uncover a number. Which picture has that number of dots in all? Point to it. Say the doubles-plus-2 fact for those dots.

Use your square to cover the addends on the left. Repeat until every number in the right column is uncovered.

12
14
4
6
10
16
18
8

Try Again This time, cover all the addends on the left. Then play the opposite way.

Look and See

Partner Talk
Share your thinking while you work.

Start Put  in a .

Get 20 squares. Pretend the squares are crackers.
Put them on the plate after you read the story. Take turns.

Try Pick 2 tiles. Put them in the story. Read the story.
Ask your partner to answer questions **a** and **b**.

Rebecca puts ☐ crackers on a plate.

Then Betty puts ☐ more crackers on a plate.

a.
How many crackers did Rebecca and Betty put on the plate?

b.
How many crackers are left after Betty eats 2 crackers?

Try Again Put your tiles back in the .
Repeat until each player makes five stories.

Center Activity ⭐ 5-4

Look and See

Partner Talk

Share your thinking while you work.

Start ✷ Put 2 3 4 5 6 7 8 9 in a 🛍.

Get 20 squares. Pretend the squares are butterflies.
Put them in the garden after you read the story.

Try Pick 2 tiles. Put them in the story. Read the story.
Ask your partner to answer each question.

10 butterflies are in the garden.  more join them.

How many butterflies are there altogether?

Later,  butterflies leave the garden.

How many butterflies are still in the garden?

Try Again Put your tiles back in the 🛍.
Repeat until each player makes five stories.

Try Together

Start 👫 Get a 🎲. Get 9 red squares. Get 9 blue squares.
Take turns until each of you gets 5 turns.

Try Toss the 🎲. Follow the directions.
Then ask your partner to move some blue squares
to the top ten-frame to make 10.

🎲	Show 8 red squares and 3 blue squares.	🎲	Show 9 red squares and 4 blue squares.
🎲	Show 9 red squares and 6 blue squares.	🎲	Show 7 red squares and 5 blue squares.
🎲	Show 8 red squares and 6 blue squares.	🎲	Show 7 red squares and 6 blue squares.

Red Squares

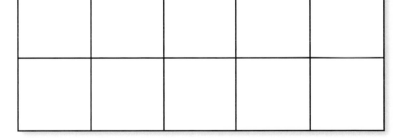

Blue Squares

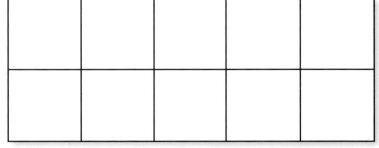

Say the two addition sentences.
For example, say $7 + 4 = 11$ and $10 + 1 = 11$.

Try Again Put some red squares in the top ten-frame.
Put some blue squares in the bottom one.
Ask your partner to add those two numbers by making 10.

Try Together

Partner Talk

Share your thinking while you work.

Start 👥 Get 17 red squares. Take turns until each of you gets 5 turns.

Try Point to a number. Get that number of squares.
Put 10 squares in the left ten-frame. Put the rest in the ten-frame on the right. Move some squares from the left to the right.
Say two addition sentences.

For example, say 10 + 1 = 11, and 9 + 2 = 11.

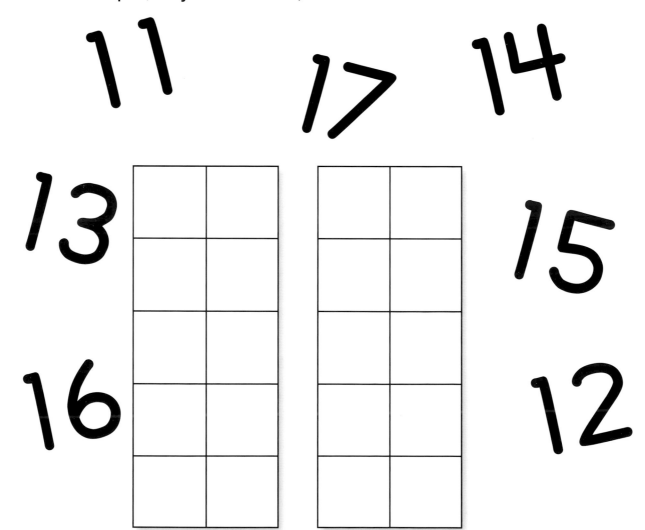

11   17   14

13   15

16   12

Try Again This time, find two other ways to show the same number of squares in all.

Center Activity ★ ★ 5-5

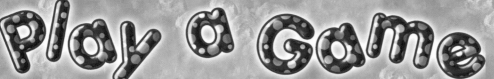

Play a Game

Partner Talk

Share your thinking while you work.

 **Start** Get a . Get 20 red squares.
Give one game board to each player. Take turns.

Try Toss the to see what number you will add to 9.
Then find an addition fact with ten that helps you get the answer.
Cover the fact if you see it on your game board.

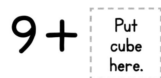

$$9 +$$ Put cube here.

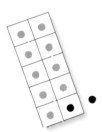
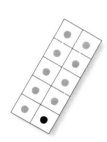

Player 1	
10 + 3	10 + 4
10 + 2	10 + 1
10 + 5	10 + 3
10 + 1	10 + 5
10 + 2	10 + 0

Player 2	
10 + 1	10 + 3
10 + 5	10 + 0
10 + 2	10 + 1
10 + 3	10 + 4
10 + 5	10 + 2

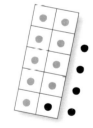
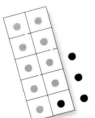
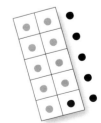

To win, cover one column on your game board!

 **Try Again** Play again!

Center Activity ★ 5-6

Play a Game

Partner Talk

Share your thinking while you work.

Start ✳ Put ①②③④⑤⑥⑦⑧ in a 🛍.

Get 20 red squares. Take turns.

Try Pick a tile. Add that number to 10. Say the sum. Find an addition fact with 9 that has the same sum. Cover the fact if you see it on your game board. Put the tile in the 🛍.

$$10 + \boxed{} \quad \text{has the same sum as } 9 + \underline{\quad}.$$

Player 1	
9 + 4	9 + 7
9 + 8	9 + 5
9 + 2	9 + 9
9 + 6	9 + 3
9 + 5	9 + 2

Player 2	
9 + 6	9 + 5
9 + 2	9 + 3
9 + 4	9 + 7
9 + 8	9 + 2
9 + 3	9 + 9

To win, cover one column on your game board!

Try Again Play again!

Center Activity ★ ★ 5-6

Play a Game

Start 👬 Put 3 4 5 6 in a 🛍️.

Get 10 blue squares for Player 1. Get 10 red squares for Player 2. Take turns until all the game spaces are covered.

Try Pick a tile. Place it next to the 8 to make an addition fact. Find an addition fact with 10 to help you add 8. If you see it on the game board, cover it with a square. Put the tile in the 🛍️.

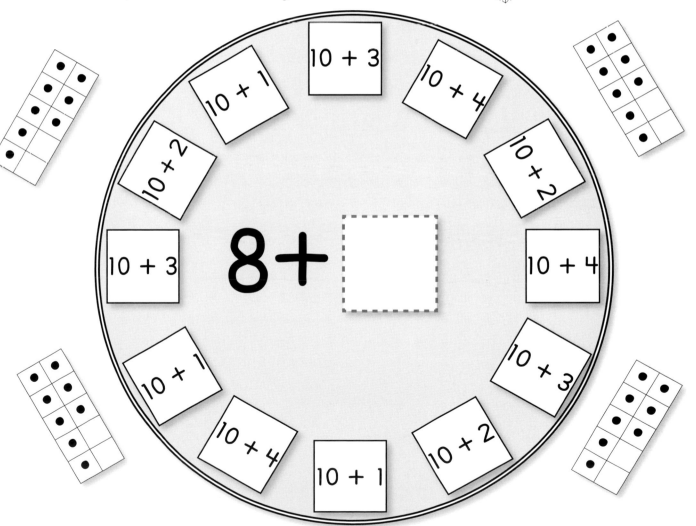

To win, cover the most game spaces.

Try Again Play again!

Play a Game

Partner Talk

Share your thinking while you work.

Start 👥 Put  1 2 3 4 5 6 7 in a 🛍.

Get 15 blue squares for Player 1.
Get 15 red squares for Player 2. Take turns.

Try Pick a tile. Place it next to the 10. Say the sum. Say an addition fact with 8 that has the same sum. If you see it on the game board, cover it with a square. Put the tile in the 🛍.

$$10 + \boxed{}$$

8 + 8	8 + 4	8 + 6	8 + 3	8 + 5	8 + 8	8 + 4
8 + 3	8 + 7	8 + 8	8 + 5	8 + 9	8 + 4	8 + 7
8 + 9	8 + 6	8 + 3	8 + 7	8 + 9	8 + 5	8 + 3

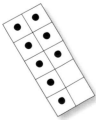

To win,
be the first player to cover 8 game spaces.

Try Again Play again!

Look and See

Partner Talk

Share your thinking while you work.

Start 🏃 Get 🎲 🎲 🎲. Take turns until you each get 5 turns.

Try Toss 🎲 🎲 🎲. Put them in the spaces below. Add two of the numbers. Let your partner add the other number. Point to the sum.

┌─────────┐   ┌─────────┐   ┌─────────┐
│ Put   │ ➕ │ Put   │ ➕ │ Put   │ =
│ cube   │   │ cube   │   │ cube   │   _____
│ here. │   │ here. │   │ here. │   Sum
└─────────┘   └─────────┘   └─────────┘

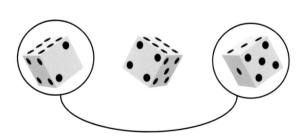

Point to the Sum

3   18   5

8   13   14

15   16   17

7   4   11

10   6   9   12

Try Again This time, make up a number story for your three numbers before you add them.

Center Activity ★ 5-8

Look and See

Partner Talk

Share your thinking while you work.

Start ☆ Get  and

1 2 3 4 5 6 7 8 9.

Get 12 squares. Cover the numbers.

Try Uncover a number. Which three numbers have this sum?
Show your answer below with tiles.
Ask your partner to show three numbers that have the same sum.
Remove the tiles. Take turns until all the numbers are uncovered.

8   15   9   13   11   17

12   7   10   18   16   14

☐ + ☐ + ☐ = ___
Sum

☐ + ☐ + ☐ = ___
Sum

Try Again Talk about which numbers you add first and why.

Center Activity ★★ 5-8

Look and See

Partner Talk

Share your thinking while you work.

Start 👥 Get 16 red squares.

Get ,

and **0 1 2 3 4 5 6 7 8 9**.

Solve. Talk about the best way to group the addends.

Try Ellen packs her toys into 3 boxes. How many toys does she have in all?

Use your squares to show a number of toys in each box.

Then use tiles to make an addition sentence.

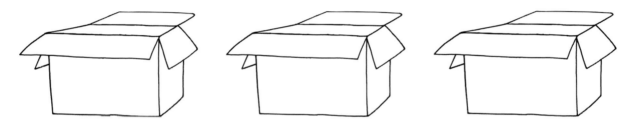

Ruby puts flowers into 3 vases. How many flowers does she have in all? Use your squares to show a number of flowers in each vase. Then use tiles to make an addition sentence.

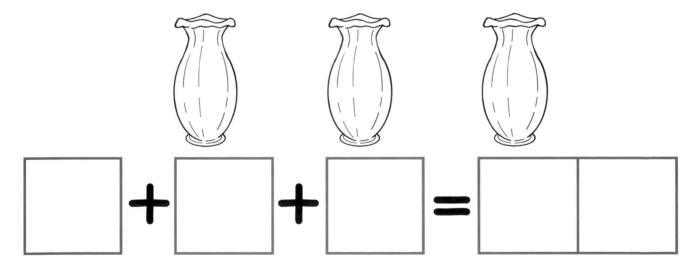

Try Again Play again! Talk about how you add three numbers.

Look and See

Start 👥 Get 18 red squares.

Get a ✏️ and a 📎 to make a spinner.

Get [0] [1] [2] [3] [4] [5] [6] [7] [8] [9] ,

[0] [1] [2] [3] [4] [5] [6] [7] [8] [9] ,

and [0] [1] [2] [3] [4] [5] [6] [7] [8] [9] .

Try Spin. Then take that number of squares. Pretend your squares are books. Put those books on an empty desk. Repeat 2 more times. Use tiles to make an addition sentence to show how many books in all. Take turns. Talk about the best way to group the addends each time.

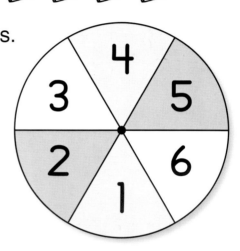

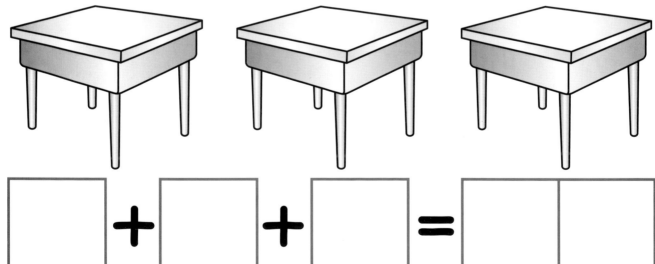

☐ **+** ☐ **+** ☐ **=** ☐☐

Try Again This time, check your answer by grouping the addends in a different way then adding.

Listen and Learn

Partner Talk

Share your thinking while you work.

Start 👫 Get 7 blue squares to cover the subtraction facts.
Get 18 red squares.
Take turns.

Try Uncover a game space. Say the subtraction fact.
Make 10 to subtract. Use red squares and the ten-frame.
Tell your partner the steps you use to subtract.

| 12 – 8 | 14 – 6 | 17 – 8 | 15 – 8 | 18 – 9 | 13 – 6 | 16 – 9 |

Cover each difference with a blue square.

| 9 | 7 | 8 | 7 | 4 | 7 | 9 |

Try Again Play again!

Listen and Learn

Start 🏃 Get a 🎲. Get 15 red squares.

Get **4** **5** **6** **7** **8** **9** . Take turns.

Try Toss the 🎲. Find your toss.
Use red squares and the ten-frame to show the number in all.
Make 10 to subtract. Tell your partner the steps you use to subtract.

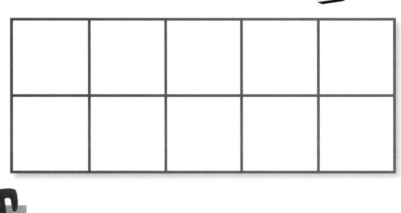

    ⚀ 14 – 8   ⚁ 12 – 5   ⚂ 11 – 6

    ⚃ 15 – 6   ⚄ 13 – 5   ⚅ 11 – 7

Use a number tile to show each difference.

Try Again Play again!

Try Together

Partner Talk

Share your thinking while you work.

Start 👫 Get 18 red squares.

Get  5 6 7 8 9 .

Try Pick a story. Read it together. Use squares and the ten-frame to subtract. Put a number tile on the story to show the answer.

A Lilly has 12 marbles. She gives 7 marbles to Tanner. How many marbles does Lilly have left?

B The pet store has 17 goldfish in a tank. Austin buys 8 of the goldfish. How many goldfish are left in the tank?

C Kimberly had a bag with 15 oranges in it. The next day the bag had 8 oranges in it. How many oranges were taken out of the bag?

D Nolan and Zoe collected 13 shells at the beach. Nolan found 5 of the shells. How many did Zoe find?

E There are 15 children in Ms. Hunter's class. Nine of the children are wearing gym shoes. How many children are not wearing gym shoes?

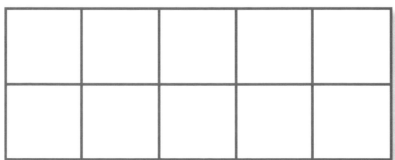

Try Again This time, tell and solve your own subtraction stories.

Try Together

Share your thinking while you work.

Start 🏃 Get 18 red squares. Get 1 blue square.

Get a ⌇ and a ✏️ to make a spinner.
Work together.

Try Choose a story. Put a blue square next to it. Spin on the top spinner. Say the subtraction fact. Spin on the bottom spinner. Name the toy. Say your numbers and your toy in the story. Use squares and the ten-frame to subtract. Answer the question.

A Taylor had _____. She gave _____ of them to Colton. How many _____ does Taylor have now?

B The store had _____ on the shelf in the morning. By the afternoon, _____ were sold. How many _____ are left on the shelf?

C There were _____ in the toy box. The children took out _____ for recess. How many _____ are left in the toy box?

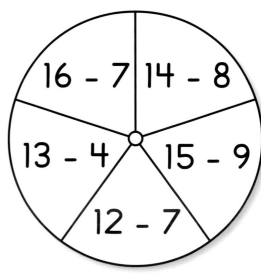

Try Again This time, say a subtraction fact that is not on the spinner. Then spin for a toy.

Helping Hands

Partner Talk — Share your thinking while you work.

Start 👫 Put 5 6 7 8 9 in a 🛍️ .

Get 17 red squares. Take turns until each player gets 5 turns.

Try Pick two tiles.
Put them in these spaces.
Use squares to show each
number on the workmat.

[ ] **+** [ ] **=** _____

Say: ____ **+** ____ **=** ____ .

Have your partner point to a related subtraction fact.

15 - 9 = 6	13 - 6 = 7	17 - 9 = 8
14 - 9 = 5	14 - 8 = 6	12 - 7 = 5
11 - 6 = 5	16 - 7 = 9	15 - 8 = 7
	13 - 5 = 8	

Try Again Point to a subtraction fact. Ask your partner to put squares
on the workmat to show the two parts of the whole amount.

Helping Hands

Partner Talk
Share your thinking while you work.

Start 👫 Get 18 red squares.
Take turns until each player gets 5 turns.

Try Put 15 squares in your hands. Drop them on the workmat.
Some will land on the beach and some in the ocean.
Make and say an addition fact with those parts.
Ask your partner to say a related subtraction fact.

Say: _____ + _____ = _____ .
        part   part   WHOLE

_____ - _____ = _____ .
WHOLE   part   part

Put a different number of squares in your hands for each turn.

Try Again This time, make a subtraction fact first.

Partner Talk

Share your thinking while you work.

Start 👫 Get 🎲 and 🎲. Get 9 red squares.
Give one game board to each player. Take turns.

Try Toss the 🎲🎲. If you see a double, toss again. Say an addition fact that has your two numbers. Look for two subtraction facts in the same fact family on your game board. If you see them, say those facts and cover them with a square. If not, lose your turn.

Put one cube here.		Put the other cube here.	=	
Number on one cube		Number on the other cube		Number in all

Player 1
Win With Five

5 - 3 = 2	7 - 5 = 2	11 - 6 = 5
5 - 2 = 3	7 - 2 = 5	11 - 5 = 6
5 - 4 = 1	9 - 5 = 4	8 - 5 = 3
5 - 1 = 4	9 - 4 = 5	8 - 3 = 5
7 - 6 = 1	7 - 4 = 3	10 - 6 = 4
7 - 1 = 6	7 - 3 = 4	10 - 4 = 6

Player 2
Win With Five

9 - 5 = 4	6 - 4 = 2	9 - 6 = 3
9 - 4 = 5	6 - 2 = 4	9 - 3 = 6
3 - 2 = 1	10 - 6 = 4	7 - 4 = 3
3 - 1 = 2	10 - 4 = 6	7 - 3 = 4
8 - 6 = 2	4 - 3 = 1	6 - 5 = 1
8 - 2 = 6	4 - 1 = 3	6 - 1 = 5

To win, be the first player to cover five game spaces.

Try Again Play again!

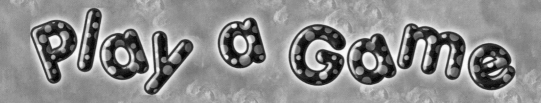

Partner Talk

Share your thinking while you work.

Start 👫 Get 🎲 and 🎲. Get 9 red squares.
Give one game board to each player. Take turns.

Try Toss the 🎲 🎲. If you see a double, toss again. Say a subtraction fact that has your two numbers. Look for two addition facts in the same fact family on your game board. If you see them, say those facts and cover them with a square. If not, lose your turn.

―――――	−	=
Number in all	Put one cube here.	Put the other cube here.
	Number on one cube	Number on the other cube

Player 1 Win With Five		
2 + 6 = 8	1 + 2 = 3	3 + 6 = 9
6 + 2 = 8	2 + 1 = 3	6 + 3 = 9
2 + 5 = 7	4 + 6 = 10	1 + 3 = 4
5 + 2 = 7	6 + 4 = 10	3 + 1 = 4
2 + 3 = 5	1 + 5 = 6	4 + 5 = 9
3 + 2 = 5	5 + 1 = 6	5 + 4 = 9

Player 2 Win With Five		
3 + 4 = 7	5 + 6 = 11	3 + 5 = 8
4 + 3 = 7	6 + 5 = 11	5 + 3 = 8
2 + 4 = 6	4 + 5 = 9	1 + 4 = 5
4 + 2 = 6	5 + 4 = 9	4 + 1 = 5
1 + 6 = 7	2 + 6 = 8	4 + 6 = 10
6 + 1 = 7	6 + 2 = 8	6 + 4 = 10

To win, be the first player to cover five game spaces.

Try Again Play again!

Cover Three

Start 👥 Put  1 2 3 4 5 6 7 8 9 in a 🛍️.

Get 6 red squares for one player.
Get 6 blue squares for the other player. Take turns.

Try Pick a tile. Find the marbles next to that number. Talk about the two parts and the whole. Look on the game board. Find two facts that match the picture. Explain how to complete each fact. Cover the facts. Set the tile aside.

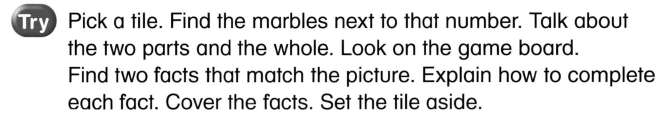

12 − 5 = __ 5 + __ = 12	13 − 4 = __ 4 + __ = 13	14 − 6 = __ 6 + __ = 14
15 − 8 = __ 8 + __ = 15	11 − 2 = __ 2 + __ = 11	16 − 7 = __ 7 + __ = 16
18 − 9 = __ 9 + __ = 18	10 − 6 = __ 6 + __ = 10	17 − 9 = __ 9 + __ = 17

To win, get: ■■■ or ■ or ■ or ■

Try Again Play again!

Cover Three

Partner Talk

Share your thinking while you work.

Start  Put   in a .

Get 6 red squares for one player.
Get 6 blue squares for the other player. Take turns.

Try Pick a tile. Find the marbles next to that number. Talk about the two parts and the whole. Look on the game board. Find a fact that matches the picture. Explain how to complete that fact. Cover the fact. Set the tile aside.

       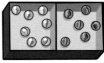

 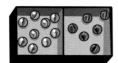

15 – 9 = __	12 – 8 = __	10 – 8 = __
18 – 9 = __	11 – 4 = __	17 – 8 = __
13 – 7 = __	16 – 7 = __	14 – 5 = __

To win, get: ■■■ or ■ or ■   or
                    ■   ■   ■
                    ■   ■   ■

Try Again Play again!

Look and See

Share your thinking while you work.

Start 🧒 Get 6 red squares. Take turns.

Try Point to a large basketball. Find a related addition fact above the net. Say both facts to your partner. At the end of your turn, cover the addition fact with a square.

$$\begin{array}{r} 8 \\ + 3 \\ \hline 11 \end{array}$$

$$\begin{array}{r} 12 \\ - 9 \\ \hline \square \end{array}$$

$$\begin{array}{r} 15 \\ - 6 \\ \hline \square \end{array}$$

$$\begin{array}{r} 14 \\ - 8 \\ \hline \square \end{array}$$

$$\begin{array}{r} 8 \\ + 8 \\ \hline 16 \end{array}$$

$$\begin{array}{r} 13 \\ - 5 \\ \hline \square \end{array}$$

$$\begin{array}{r} 5 \\ + 8 \\ \hline 13 \end{array}$$

$$\begin{array}{r} 16 \\ - 8 \\ \hline \square \end{array}$$

$$\begin{array}{r} 11 \\ - 8 \\ \hline \square \end{array}$$

$$\begin{array}{r} 9 \\ + 3 \\ \hline 12 \end{array}$$

$$\begin{array}{r} 6 \\ + 9 \\ \hline 15 \end{array}$$

$$\begin{array}{r} 8 \\ + 6 \\ \hline 14 \end{array}$$

Try Again Make sure all the addition facts are covered. Take turns. Point to a subtraction fact. Then uncover an addition fact. If the facts are related, explain why. Keep the square. If not, put the square back where it was. Play until all the addition facts are uncovered.

Center Activity ★ 6-6

Look and See

Start 🚶 Get 12 red squares. Cover the baseball mitts.
Take turns until every mitt is uncovered.

Try Point to a baseball. Say the complete subtraction fact to your partner. Uncover a mitt.

If the addition fact is related to your subtraction fact, remove the square.

If not, put the square back where it was.

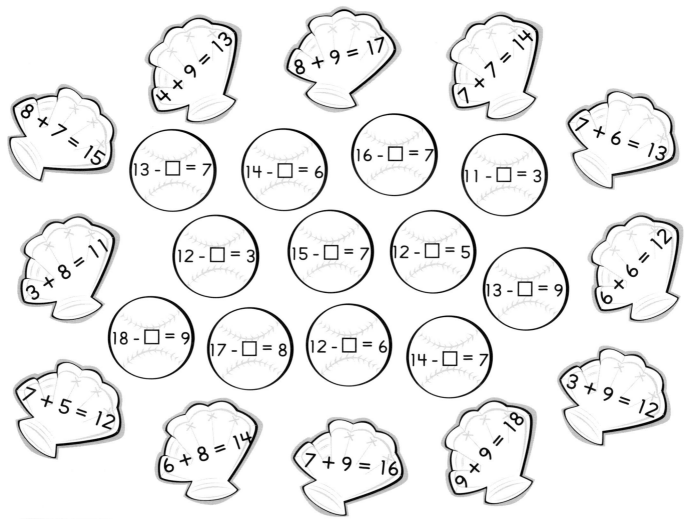

Try Again How do you decide what addition fact helps you to solve a subtraction problem?

Helping Hands

Start 🚶🚶 Get 7 red squares. Get 7 blue squares.
Pretend your squares are tickets.

Try Choose two things you would like to try at the amusement park.
Tell your partner. Count blue tickets for your first choice.
Count red tickets for your second choice. Ask your partner to say a
number sentence to show the number of tickets you need in all.

| 3 tickets | 6 tickets | 4 tickets |

| 2 tickets | 6 tickets | 4 tickets |

| 5 tickets | 7 tickets | 5 tickets |

Try Again Repeat until each player gets 5 or more turns.

Helping Hands

Start Get 🎲 🎲.
Get 12 red squares.
Pretend your squares are tickets. Take turns.

Try Toss the 🎲 🎲. Say a number sentence that shows the number of dots in all. That is the number of tickets you have to spend at the amusement park. Choose one thing to ride or buy. Say a number sentence that shows how many tickets you will have left.
What else can you buy?

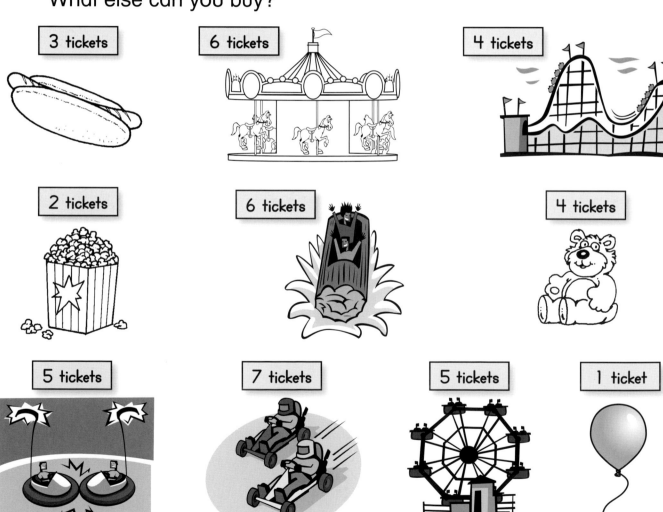

3 tickets	6 tickets	4 tickets
2 tickets	6 tickets	4 tickets
5 tickets	7 tickets	5 tickets	1 ticket

Try Again Repeat until each player gets 5 or more turns.

Look and See

Partner Talk

Share your thinking while you work.

Start 👫 Put 19 red squares in a . Take turns.

Try Take more than 10 squares from the 🛍 .
Put the squares in the ten-frames.
Say that number.
Describe that number as 10 and _____ ones.
Put the squares back in the 🛍 . Repeat.

15 FIFTEEN

17 SEVENTEEN

11 ELEVEN

14 FOURTEEN

16 SIXTEEN

18 EIGHTEEN

12 TWELVE

19 NINETEEN

13 THIRTEEN

Try Again Talk about how a dozen would look in ten-frames.

Center Activity ★ 7-1

Look and See

Partner Talk
Share your thinking while you work.

Start 👥 Get 20 red squares. Take turns.

Try Point to a number name.
Have your partner describe that number as 10 and _____ ones.
Put that number of squares in the ten-frames.
Say that number.
Put the squares back in the 🛍.
Repeat for each number name.

FIFTEEN   SEVENTEEN

ELEVEN   TWELVE

SIXTEEN   NINETEEN

FOURTEEN   EIGHTEEN   THIRTEEN

Try Again Talk about what the number 20 would look like in the ten-frames. What if you had 2 tens and some ones?

Partner Talk

Share your thinking while you work.

Start 👥 Get 14 blue squares to cover the snails. Get 18 red squares. Give one game board to each player. Take turns.

Try Uncover a snail.
Say the number that is two more than the number you uncover.
Any player who has the number you say
can cover it with a red square.
Repeat until one player wins.

16 11 17 13 4 12 15

9 14 7 10 5 8 6

Cover Nine

17	12	15
9	13	6
16	10	8

Cover Nine

18	10	19
8	11	7
9	14	6

To win, be the first player to cover nine game spaces.

Try Again Play again!

Play a Game

Start 🏃 Get 14 blue squares to cover the snails. Get 18 red squares. Give one game board to each player. Take turns.

Try Uncover a snail.
Say the number that is two less than the number you uncover.
Any player who has the number you say
can cover it with a red square.
Repeat until one player wins.

Cover Nine

14	10	6
17	9	8
12	7	11

Cover Nine

16	12	5
14	15	9
4	8	13

To win, be the first player to cover nine game spaces.

Try Again Play again! This time say the number that is one less than the number you uncover.

Partner Talk
Share your thinking while you work.

Start 👫 Get 12 red squares.
Cover each game space with a square. Take turns.

Try Uncover two game spaces.

If you find a number and its matching word name, keep the squares.

If not, put the squares back where they were.

Take turns until all the spaces are uncovered.

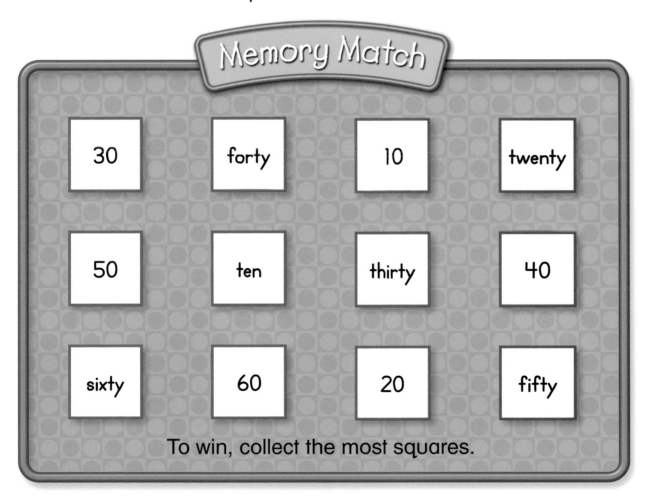

Memory Match

30	forty	10	twenty
50	ten	thirty	40
sixty	60	20	fifty

To win, collect the most squares.

Try Again Play again!

    1

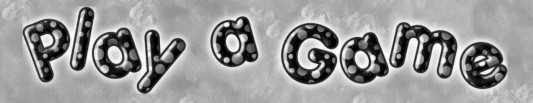

Share your thinking while you work.

Start 👫 Get 12 red squares.
Cover each game space with a square. Take turns.

Try Uncover three game spaces.

If you find three ways to write the same number, keep the squares.

If not, put the squares back where they were.

Take turns until all the spaces are uncovered.

Memory Match

7 tens	thirty	9 tens	50
90	5 tens	70	3 tens
fifty	seventy	30	ninety

To win, collect the most squares.

Try Again Play again! Or, make up your own Memory Match game.

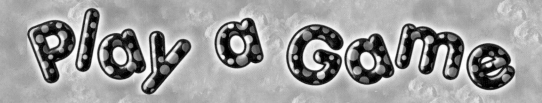

Play a Game

Partner Talk

Share your thinking while you work.

Start 🏃 Get 12 red squares.
Cover each game space with a square. Take turns.

Try Uncover two game spaces.

If you find a number and the next 3 numbers counting forward, keep the squares.

If not, put the squares back where they were.

Take turns until all the spaces are uncovered.

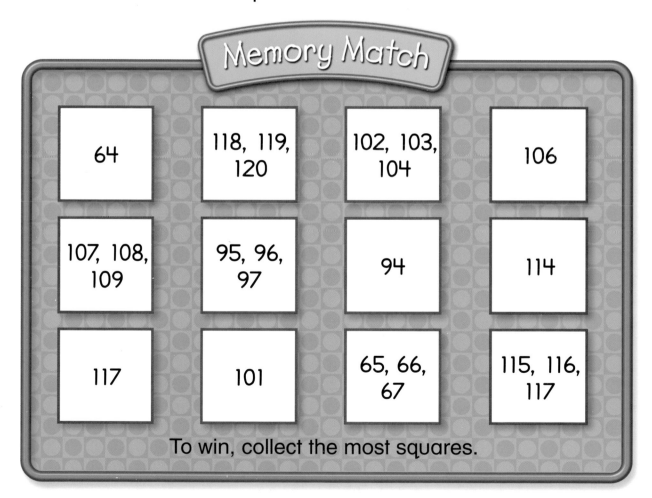

Memory Match

64	118, 119, 120	102, 103, 104	106
107, 108, 109	95, 96, 97	94	114
117	101	65, 66, 67	115, 116, 117

To win, collect the most squares.

Try Again Play again!

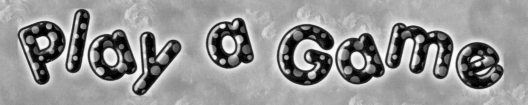

Start 🏃 Get 12 red squares.

Cover each game space with a square. Take turns.

Try Uncover two game spaces.

If you find a number and the next 3 numbers counting forward, keep the squares.

If not, put the squares back where they were.

Take turns until all the spaces are uncovered.

Memory Match

108	98	78	110
99, 100, 101	100	49	111, 112, 113
79, 80, 81	101, 102, 103	109, 110, 111	50, 51, 52

To win, collect the most squares.

Try Again Play again! Or, make up your own Memory Match game.

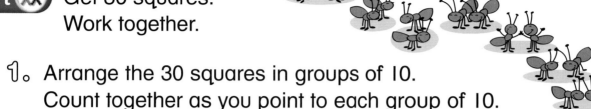

Helping Hands

Partner Talk

Share your thinking while you work.

Start 👫 Get 30 squares.
Work together.

Try 1. Arrange the 30 squares in groups of 10.
Count together as you point to each group of 10.

2. Arrange the 30 squares in groups of 2.
Count together as you point to each group of 2.

Try Again Talk about how counting by 10s can help you to add quickly.

Helping Hands

Start 👫 Get 30 squares.
Work together.

Try 1. Arrange the 30 squares in groups of 10.
Count together by 10s. Then count back to 0.

2. Arrange the 30 squares in groups of 5.
Count together by 5s. Then count back to 0.

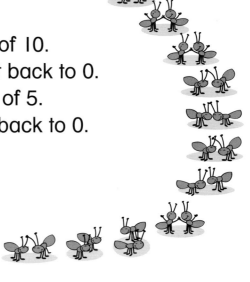

Try Again This time, try to count back to 0 faster.

Center Activity ★ ★ 7-5

Partner Talk

Share your thinking while you work.

 **Start** Work together.

 Try Choose a table. Talk about the pattern.
Say the next two numbers in the second row. Try every table.

Number of Fish	1	2	3	4	5
Number of Stripes in All	2	4	6		

Number of Bunches	1	2	3	4	5
Number of Grapes in All	10	20	30		

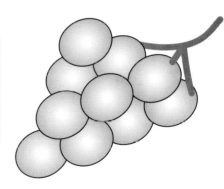

Try Again This time, take turns. Ask your partner to answer a question. For example, ask: If there are 20 balls in the air, how many jugglers are juggling?

Center Activity ⭐ **7-6**

Try Together

Start 👫 Get ⓪ ① ② ③ ④ ⑤ ⑥ ⑦ ⑧ ⑨ and

⓪ ① ② ③ ④ ⑤ ⑥ ⑦ ⑧ ⑨ . Work together.

Try Choose a table. Talk about the pattern.
Show the missing numbers with tiles below.

Each goody bag has: 2 masks, and 10 stickers.

Number of Bags	1	2	3	4	5	6	7
Number of Masks	2	4	6	8		12	

Number of Bags	1	2	3	4	5	6	7
Number of Stickers	10		30	40		60	70

[ ] bags

[|] goodies

Try Again Use tiles to show a number of bags and the number of goodies in those bags. Ask your partner to tell if the goodies are masks or stickers.

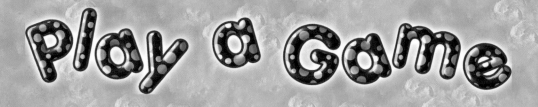

Partner Talk

Share your thinking while you work.

Start 👫 Get 12 red squares.
Cover each game space with a square.
Take turns.

Try Uncover two game spaces.

If you see a picture that matches a number, keep the squares.

If not, put the squares back where they were.

Take turns until all the spaces are uncovered.

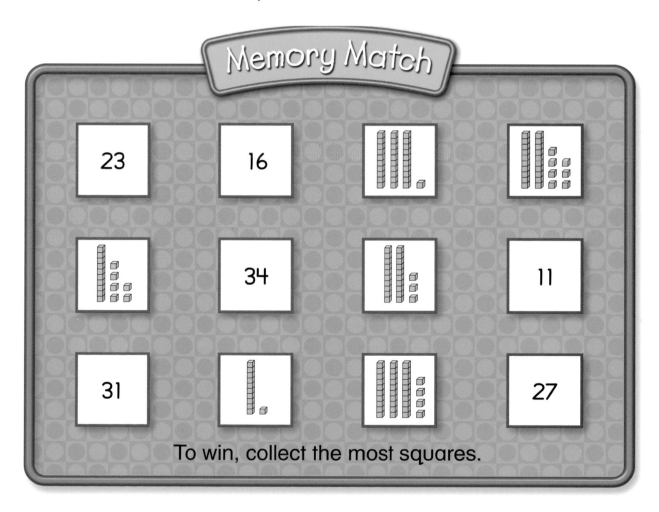

Memory Match

23	16		
34			11
31			27

To win, collect the most squares.

Try Again Play again!

Play a Game

Partner Talk

Share your thinking while you work.

Start 👫 Get 12 red squares. Cover each game space with a square. Take turns.

Try Uncover two game spaces.

If you find a number in one space, and pictures or words for that number in the other space, keep the squares. Say the tens and the ones left over to your partner.

If not, put the squares back where they were.

Take turns until all the spaces are uncovered.

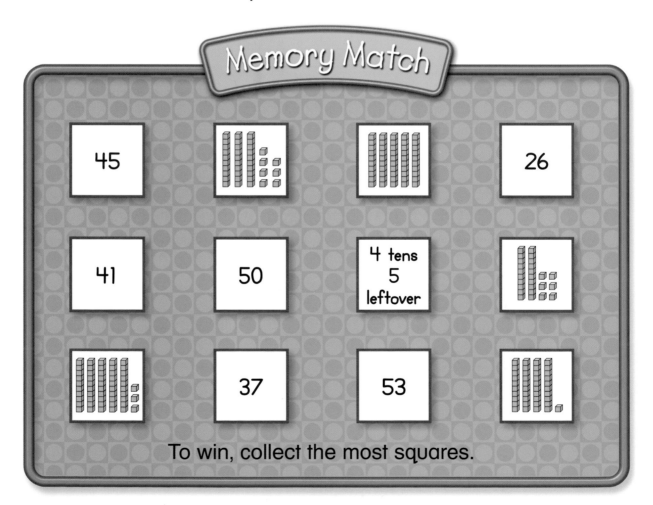

Memory Match

45 | | | 26

41 | 50 | 4 tens 5 leftover |

| 37 | 53 |

To win, collect the most squares.

Try Again Play again! Talk about why 50 is different.

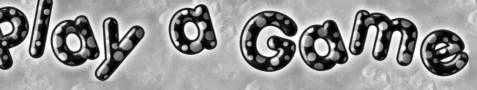

Start Put ⓵ ② ③ ④ ⑤ ⑥ in a .

Get 1 red square for one player.
Get 1 blue square for the other player. Take turns.

Try Pick a tile. Count by tens. Count that number of tens to your partner. How many numbers did you say?
Move your square forward that number of spaces on the game board. Put the tile back in the .

Start Here! →

To win, get to the star!

★

Try Again Play again! Talk about things in the classroom that you can count by tens.

Play a Game

Start Put  in a 🛍.

Get 1 red square for one player.
Get 1 blue square for the other player. Take turns.

Try Pick a tile. Count by tens. Count that number of tens to your partner.
How many numbers did you say?
Move your square forward that number of spaces on
the game board. Put the tile back in the 🛍.

Start
Here!
→

| | | Count by tens to 100. | | | | Count back by tens from 30. |

To win, get to the star!

| | | Count back by tens from 60. | | | Say one ten less than 50. | |

You're almost there!

★

| | | | Say two tens more than 70. | | |

Try Again Play again! How are counting dimes and
counting by tens alike? Talk about it.

Helping Hands

Start  Get ⓪ ① ② ③ ④ ⑤ ⑥ ⑦ ⑧ ⑨ .

Take turns.

Try Point to a rectangle. Read the number of tens and ones.

Say to your partner: "Please put tiles on the workmat to show this number."

Ask your partner to say that number.

Six tens Five ones	Four tens Three ones	Two tens One one

Seven tens Zero ones	Three tens Eight ones	Five tens Four ones	One tens Nine ones

Workmat

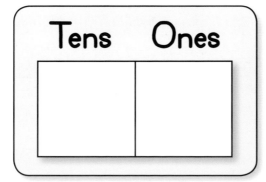

Tens	Ones

Try Again Talk about what would happen if you put the two tiles in a different order.

Center Activity ★ 8-3

Helping Hands

Start 👫 Get 0 1 2 3 4 5 6 7 8 9 . Take turns.

Try Pick one rectangle. Do not tell your partner which one.
Put tiles on the workmat. Show that number of tens and ones.
Ask your partner to point to your rectangle.
Talk about why that number matches the words in the rectangle.

Three ones Six tens	Four tens Eight ones	Five tens One one

Nine tens Seven ones	Three ones Two tens	Eight tens Three ones	Seven ones Five tens

Seven tens Nine ones	Three tens Eight ones	Two ones Three tens

Workmat

Tens	Ones

Try Again Name numbers that have more than 5 tens.

Share your thinking while you work.

Start Get 18 red squares. Cover every robot's number and every star with a square. Take turns.

Try Uncover one robot's number and one star. If both numbers match, keep the squares. If not, put the squares back.

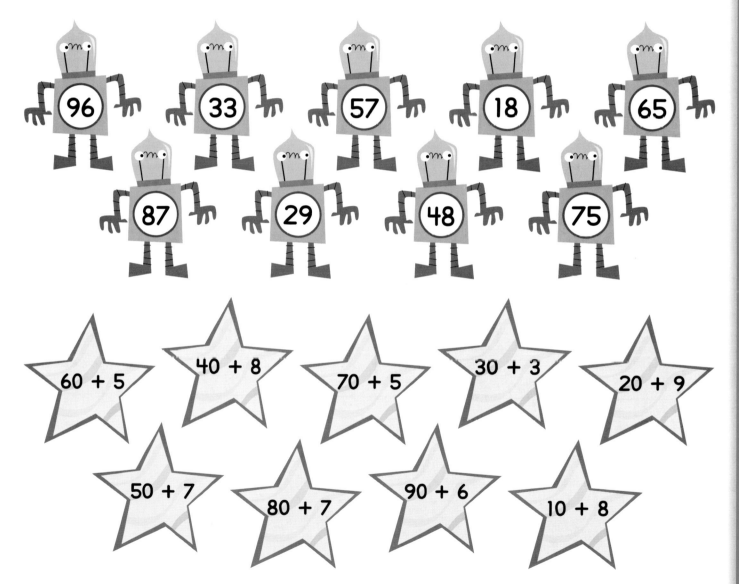

96 33 57 18 65

87 29 48 75

60 + 5   40 + 8   70 + 5   30 + 3   20 + 9

50 + 7   80 + 7   90 + 6   10 + 8

When all the robots and stars are uncovered,
the player with the most squares wins!

Try Again Play again! This time count by tens and ones to make the number on the star.

    1

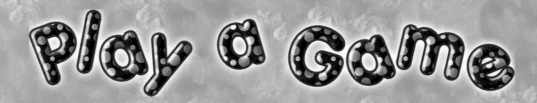

Partner Talk

Share your thinking while you work.

Start 🚶 Get 18 red squares. Cover every planet and every comet with a square. Take turns.

Try Uncover a planet and a comet. Say the numbers in expanded form. Example: "80 plus 6."
If the number you said in expanded form matches the number on a star, keep the squares. If not, put the squares back.

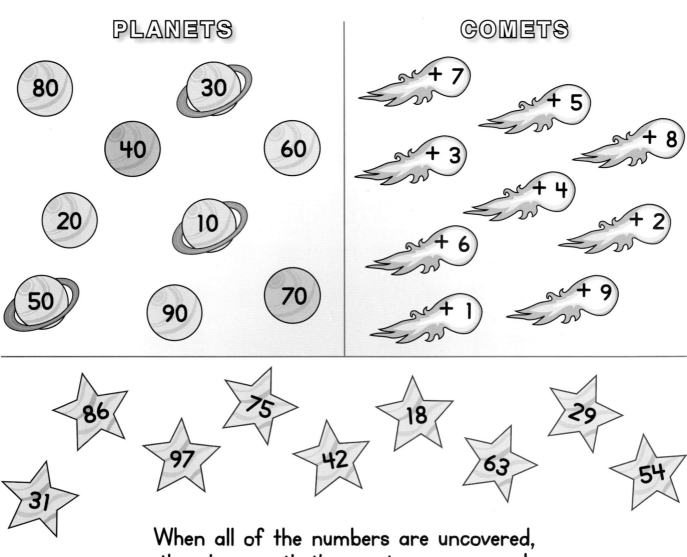

PLANETS

80   30   40   60   20   10   50   90   70

COMETS

+7   +5   +3   +8   +4   +6   +2   +1   +9

86   75   18   29   97   42   63   54   31

When all of the numbers are uncovered, the player with the most squares wins!

Try Again Play again! This time, say a number on a star first, and then uncover a planet and a comet.

Look and See

Partner Talk

Share your thinking while you work.

Start 👥 Put 40 squares in a 🛍️. Look at the 23 boxes on the dock. Then look at the boats. Talk about ways to make 23 with tens and ones.

Try Take a handful of squares from the 🛍️. Count them. Pretend your squares are boxes. Stack the boxes on the dock. Fill as many boats as you can. After you fill each boat, tell how many tens are in the boats and how many ones are on the dock. Remove the squares. Repeat five or more times.

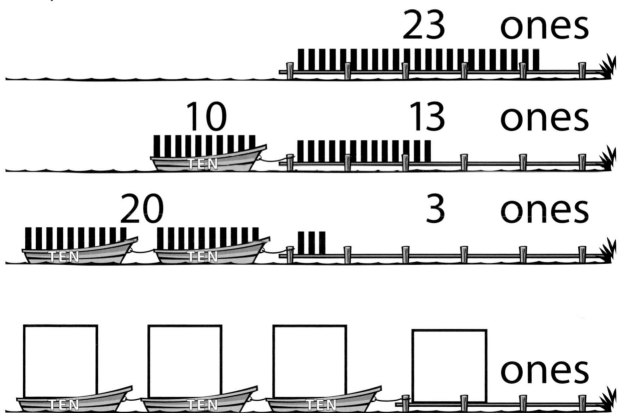

Try Again This time, take two handfuls of squares from the 🛍️. Fill as many boats as you can with ten boxes. Put any extra boxes on the dock. Tell how many boxes you have. Unload the boats one at a time. After you unload each boat, tell how many tens are in the boats, and how many ones are on the dock.

Look and See

Partner Talk
Share your thinking while you work.

Start 🚶 Get a 🎲 and a ✏️ .
Take turns until each player gets 5 turns.

Try Toss the 🎲 . Find the tens and ones next to your toss. Say that number. Place a pencil to the right of a ten tower. Say another way to make your number with tens and ones. Remember, you can break apart a ten to get ones.

Try Again This time, find all the ways to make each number. Remember, you can break apart tens to get ones.

Start 👥 Get a 🎲. Get 18 red squares. Get 📝.
Give one game board to each player. Take turns.

Try Toss the 🎲. Find your toss in the table. Cover a space on the game board that shows a way to make the number next to your toss.
If you do not see a way to make that number, lose your turn.

Toss	Cover a Way to Make
⚀	56
⚁	37
⚂	24

Toss	Cover a Way to Make
⚃	43
⚄	28
⚅	62

Four Corners

1 ten 27 ones	3 tens 26 ones	6 tens 2 ones
4 tens 3 ones	2 tens 4 ones	2 tens 17 ones
2 tens 23 ones	1 ten 18 ones	5 tens 6 ones

Four Corners

4 tens 16 ones	5 tens 6 ones	3 tens 13 ones
1 ten 33 ones	3 tens 7 ones	5 tens 12 ones
4 tens 22 ones	1 ten 14 ones	2 tens 8 ones

To win, be the first player who covers four corners.

Try Again Toss the 🎲.
Make a list of three ways to get the number next to your toss.

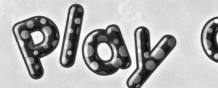 # Play a Game

Start 🏃 Get a 🎲. Get 18 red squares. Get 📝.
Give one game board to each player. Take turns.

Try Toss the 🎲. Find your toss in the table. Cover a space on the game board that shows another way to make the number next to your toss. If you do not see another way to make that number, lose your turn.

Toss	Cover a Way to Make
⚀	7 tens 14 ones
⚁	5 tens 26 ones
⚂	4 tens 12 ones

Toss	Cover a Way to Make
⚃	1 ten 36 ones
⚄	6 tens 15 ones
⚅	2 tens 38 ones

Four Corners

8 tens 4 ones	7 tens 5 ones	2 tens 26 ones
5 tens 34 ones	4 tens 36 ones	3 tens 28 ones
4 tens 35 ones	4 tens 6 ones	3 tens 22 ones

Four Corners

3 tens 16 ones	5 tens 2 ones	6 tens 24 ones
6 tens 16 ones	7 tens 6 ones	1 ten 48 ones
2 tens 32 ones	5 tens 8 ones	5 tens 25 ones

To win, be the first player who covers four corners.

Try Again Toss the 🎲. Make a list of three other ways to get the number next to your toss.

Look and See

Partner Talk

Share your thinking while you work.

Start Get 6 red squares. Take turns.

Try Point to a flower.
Follow directions. When you finish, put a red square on it.
Repeat until all the flowers are covered.

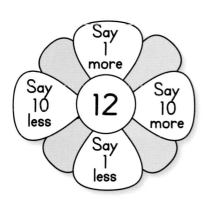

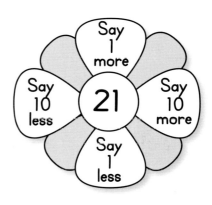

1	2	3	4	5	6	7	8	9	10
11	12	13	14	15	16	17	18	19	20
21	22	23	24	25	26	27	28	29	30
31	32	33	34	35	36	37	38	39	40
41	42	43	44	45	46	47	48	49	50

Try Again Take turns. Point to any number in the chart. Follow directions on the flower petals for your number.

Look and See

Start Put 0 1 2 3 4 5 6 7 8 9 in a 🛍.

Take turns.

Try Pick two tiles. Put them in the empty spaces.
Follow directions. Put the tiles back in the 🛍.
Repeat until each player gets 5 turns.

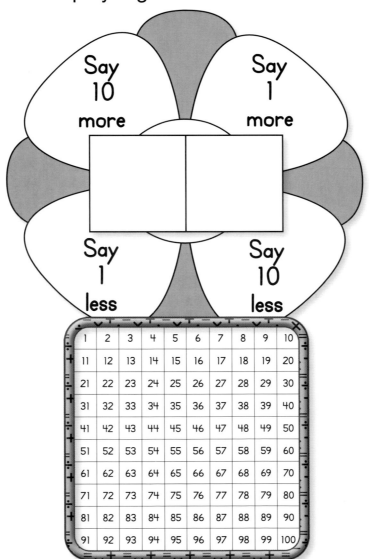

Say 10 more

Say 1 more

Say 1 less

Say 10 less

1	2	3	4	5	6	7	8	9	10
11	12	13	14	15	16	17	18	19	20
21	22	23	24	25	26	27	28	29	30
31	32	33	34	35	36	37	38	39	40
41	42	43	44	45	46	47	48	49	50
51	52	53	54	55	56	57	58	59	60
61	62	63	64	65	66	67	68	69	70
71	72	73	74	75	76	77	78	79	80
81	82	83	84	85	86	87	88	89	90
91	92	93	94	95	96	97	98	99	100

Try Again Take turns. Point to any number in the chart. Follow
directions on the flower petals for your number.

Look and See

Partner Talk
Share your thinking while you work.

Start 🕅 Put  **0 1 2 3 4 5 6 7 8** in a .

Get a 🎲. Take turns until each partner gets 5 or more turns.

Try Pick two tiles. Put the tiles in the empty spaces. Say that number. Toss the 🎲. Read the directions next to your toss.

⚀	Point to and say the number that is one more than the number you chose.
⚁	Point to and say the number that is ten less than the number you chose.
⚂	Point to and say the number that is one less than the number you chose.

⚁	Point to and say the number that is ten more than the number you chose.
⚄	Point to and say all the numbers that are in the same row as the number you chose.
⚅	Point to and say all the numbers that are in the same column as the number you chose.

Try Again Begin again! This time, try to give your answer without looking at the hundred chart.

Look and See

Partner Talk
Share your thinking while you work.

Start 👥 Get 0 1 2 3 4 5 6 7 8 9
and 0 1 2 3 4 5 6 7 8 9.

Get a 🎲. Take turns until each partner gets 5 or more turns.

Try Toss the 🎲. Read the riddle next to that toss. Solve it. Put tiles in the empty spaces to show the answer. Ask your partner to check by using the hundred chart.

1	2	3	4	5	6	7	8	9	10
11	12	13	14	15	16	17	18	19	20
21	22	23	24	25	26	27	28	29	30
31	32	33	34	35	36	37	38	39	40
41	42	43	44	45	46	47	48	49	50
51	52	53	54	55	56	57	58	59	60
61	62	63	64	65	66	67	68	69	70
71	72	73	74	75	76	77	78	79	80
81	82	83	84	85	86	87	88	89	90
91	92	93	94	95	96	97	98	99	100

⚀	This number is ten less than 57.
⚁	This number is one more than 75.
⚂	This number is one less than 99.

⚀	This number is ten more than 87.
⚁	This number is twenty less than 52.
⚂	This number is twenty more than 30.

Try Again Take turns. This time, make up a riddle for your partner. Ask your partner to put tiles in the empty spaces to show the answer.

Cover Three

Start 👫 Put  **0 1 2 3 4 5 6 7 8 9** in a .

Get 6 red squares. Get 6 blue squares. Take turns.

Try Pick two tiles. Make a two-digit number. Say that number. Do you see a number greater than your number on the game board?

If **YES**, put a square on it.

If **NO**, lose your turn.

Put the tiles back in the 🛍. Take turns until one player wins.

42	18	36
39	57	91
64	48	72

To win, get: ■■■ or ■ or ■ or
⬛
⬛ ⬛ ⬛
⬛ ⬛ ⬛ ⬛

Try Again Play again! This time, find a number that is less than your number.

Cover Three

Partner Talk

Share your thinking while you work.

Start 👫 Put  0 1 2 3 4 5 6 7 8 9 in a .

Get 6 red squares. Get 6 blue squares. Take turns.

Try Pick two tiles. Make a two-digit number. Say that number. Look at the game board. Can you find a sentence that matches your number?

If **YES**, say that sentence and put a square on it.

If **NO**, lose your turn. Put the tiles back in the .

Take turns until one player wins.

My number is less than 50.	My number is greater than 11.	My number is less than 39.
My number is greater than 45.	My number is less than 70.	My number is greater than 27
My number is less than 80.	My number is greater than 62.	My number is less than 98.

To win, get: ■■■ or ■ or ■ or ■
                        ■   ■   ■   ■
                        ■   ■

Try Again Remove your squares. Play again.

Look and See

Partner Talk

Share your thinking while you work.

 Put ⬚0 ⬚1 ⬚2 ⬚3 ⬚4 ⬚5 ⬚6 ⬚7 ⬚8 ⬚9 in a 🛍️.

Take turns until each of you gets 5 turns.

Try Take 4 tiles from the 🛍️. Show 2 two-digit numbers.
Point to those numbers on the hundred chart.
Let your partner move the tiles to form a number sentence that
is true. Take turns reading the number sentence aloud. Put the
tiles in the 🛍️.

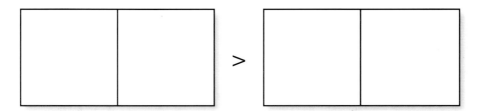

1	2	3	4	5	6	7	8	9	10
11	12	13	14	15	16	17	18	19	20
21	22	23	24	25	26	27	28	29	30
31	32	33	34	35	36	37	38	39	40
41	42	43	44	45	46	47	48	49	50
51	52	53	54	55	56	57	58	59	60
61	62	63	64	65	66	67	68	69	70
71	72	73	74	75	76	77	78	79	80
81	82	83	84	85	86	87	88	89	90
91	92	93	94	95	96	97	98	99	100

Try Again How can you use the hundred chart to tell which of your
numbers is greater?

Center Activity ★ 9-4

Look and See

Start 👥 Put  and 0 1 2 3 4 5 6 7 8 9 in a 🛍️.

Take turns until each of you gets 5 turns.

Try Take 4 tiles from the 🛍️. Place them in the spaces above the chart to show a number sentence that is true. Show the number that is less first. Have your partner place the same numbers below the chart to form a different true number sentence. Take turns reading your number sentences aloud. Put the tiles in the 🛍️.

⬜⬜ > ⬜⬜

1	2	3	4	5	6	7	8	9	10
11	12	13	14	15	16	17	18	19	20
21	22	23	24	25	26	27	28	29	30
31	32	33	34	35	36	37	38	39	40
41	42	43	44	45	46	47	48	49	50
51	52	53	54	55	56	57	58	59	60
61	62	63	64	65	66	67	68	69	70
71	72	73	74	75	76	77	78	79	80
81	82	83	84	85	86	87	88	89	90
91	92	93	94	95	96	97	98	99	100

⬜⬜ < ⬜⬜

Try Again This time, point to your numbers in the hundred chart as you say them. How can you describe where the greater numbers are on the hundred chart?

Center Activity ★ ★ 9-4

Listen and Learn

Share your thinking while you work.

Start Get a 🎲. Take turns.

Try Toss the 🎲. Follow directions.

🎲	Say the first five numbers in one row.
🎲	Say the first five numbers in one column.
🎲	Say the two middle numbers in one row.

🎲	Say the last five numbers in one row.
🎲	Say the last five numbers in one column.
🎲	Say the first and last numbers in one row.

1	2	3	4	5	6	7	8	9	10
11	12	13	14	15	16	17	18	19	20
21	22	23	24	25	26	27	28	29	30
31	32	33	34	35	36	37	38	39	40
41	42	43	44	45	46	47	48	49	50
51	52	53	54	55	56	57	58	59	60
61	62	63	64	65	66	67	68	69	70
71	72	73	74	75	76	77	78	79	80
81	82	83	84	85	86	87	88	89	90
91	92	93	94	95	96	97	98	99	100

Try Again Take turns until each player gets 5 or more turns.

Listen and Learn

Partner Talk
Share your thinking while you work.

Start Get 🎲 🎲. Take turns.

Try Toss the . Use one row in each table.

Toss	Look at the numbers between
⚀	25 and 65
⚁	40 and 70
⚂	20 and 40
⚃	10 and 30
⚄	15 and 45
⚅	65 and 95

Toss	Say
⚀	the odd numbers
⚁	the even numbers
⚂	the numbers with 5 in the ones place
⚃	the numbers with 0 in the ones place
⚄	the numbers with 9 in the ones place
⚅	the numbers with 4 in the ones place

1	2	3	4	5	6	7	8	9	10
11	12	13	14	15	16	17	18	19	20
21	22	23	24	25	26	27	28	29	30
31	32	33	34	35	36	37	38	39	40
41	42	43	44	45	46	47	48	49	50
51	52	53	54	55	56	57	58	59	60
61	62	63	64	65	66	67	68	69	70
71	72	73	74	75	76	77	78	79	80
81	82	83	84	85	86	87	88	89	90
91	92	93	94	95	96	97	98	99	100

Try Again Take turns until each player gets 5 or more turns.

Center Activity ★ ★ 9-5

Share your thinking while you work.

Start 👥 Get 12 red squares.
Cover each game space with a square.
Take turns.

Try Uncover two game spaces.

If you see two ways to add the same numbers, say the sum.
Keep the squares.

If not, put the squares back where they were.

Take turns until all the spaces are uncovered.

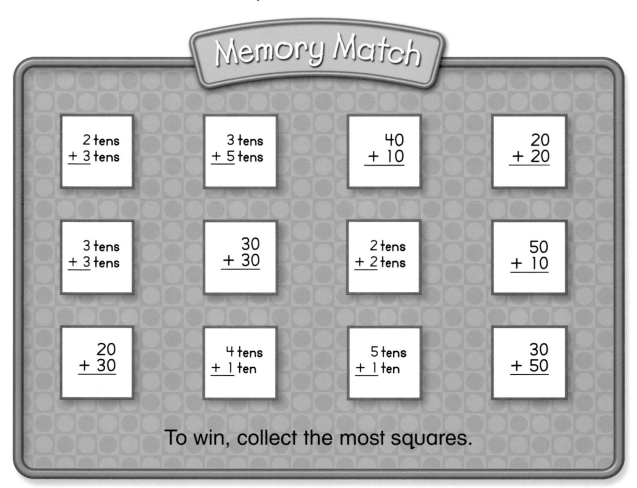

Memory Match

2 tens + 3 tens	3 tens + 5 tens	40 + 10	20 + 20
3 tens + 3 tens	30 + 30	2 tens + 2 tens	50 + 10
20 + 30	4 tens + 1 ten	5 tens + 1 ten	30 + 50

To win, collect the most squares.

Try Again Play again!

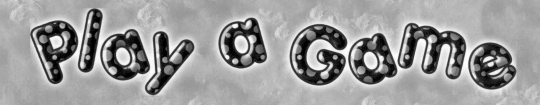

Share your thinking while you work.

Center Activity **10-1**

Start Get 12 red squares.
Cover each game space with a square.
Take turns.

Try Uncover two game spaces.

If you see two ways to add the same numbers,
say the sum. Keep the squares.

If not, put the squares back where they were.

Take turns until all the spaces are uncovered.

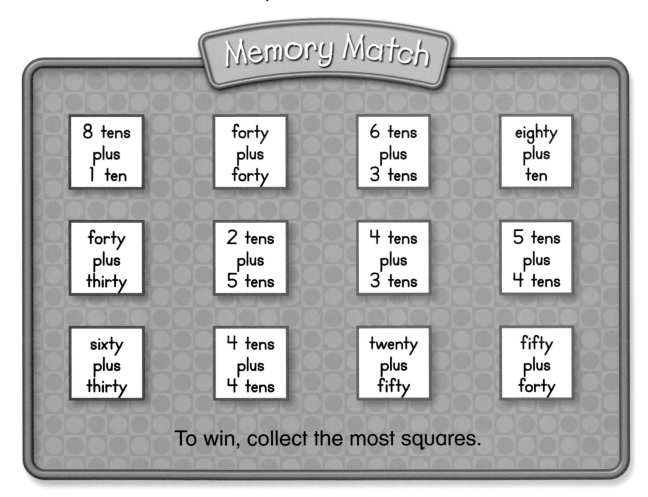

Memory Match

8 tens plus 1 ten	forty plus forty	6 tens plus 3 tens	eighty plus ten
forty plus thirty	2 tens plus 5 tens	4 tens plus 3 tens	5 tens plus 4 tens
sixty plus thirty	4 tens plus 4 tens	twenty plus fifty	fifty plus forty

To win, collect the most squares.

Try Again Play again!

Center Activity ★ ★ **10-1**

Helping Hands

Start 🏃 Get a 🎲.
Take turns.

Try Point to a number above the chart. Let your partner toss the 🎲 and tell you how many tens to add to your number. Show how to add those tens to your number on the hundred chart.

15   33   11   29

18   26   7   30

2   24

1	2	3	4	5	6	7	8	9	10
11	12	13	14	15	16	17	18	19	20
21	22	23	24	25	26	27	28	29	30
31	32	33	34	35	36	37	38	39	40
41	42	43	44	45	46	47	48	49	50
51	52	53	54	55	56	57	58	59	60
61	62	63	64	65	66	67	68	69	70
71	72	73	74	75	76	77	78	79	80
81	82	83	84	85	86	87	88	89	90
91	92	93	94	95	96	97	98	99	100

Try Again Repeat until you use every number above the chart.
Then start again using any number that is less than 40.

Helping Hands

Partner Talk

Share your thinking while you work.

Start 👥 Put 2 3 4 in a 🛍️. Take turns.

Try Point to a number above the chart. Let your partner pick a tile and tell you how many tens to add to your number.
Say the sum. Put the tile in the 🛍️.

44 57 56 4 16

1 37 40

22

32

51 19

8

1	2	3	4	5	6	7	8	9	10
11	12	13	14	15	16	17	18	19	20
21	22	23	24	25	26	27	28	29	30
31	32	33	34	35	36	37	38	39	40
41	42	43	44	45	46	47	48	49	50
51	52	53	54	55	56	57	58	59	60
61	62	63	64	65	66	67	68	69	70
71	72	73	74	75	76	77	78	79	80
81	82	83	84	85	86	87	88	89	90
91	92	93	94	95	96	97	98	99	100

Try Again Repeat until you use every number above the chart.
Then start again using any number that is less than 60.

Center Activity ★ ★ 10-2

Look and See

Partner Talk
Share your thinking while you work.

Start 🏃 Get 1 red square. Get 1 blue square.
Find out how many beads are in each group.
Take turns.

Try Use the corner of the red square.
Point to any number of beads on the
left side of the string.
Say that number.

Let your partner add
20 more beads and point
to the answer with the
blue square.

Start here

Say an addition
sentence that shows
what you and your
partner did.

Repeat until each partner gets 3 turns.

Try Again This time, add 30 more beads.
Talk about ways to add 10, for example 3 and 7.

Center Activity ★ 10-3

Look and See

Partner Talk
Share your thinking while you work.

Start Get 1 red square. Get 1 blue square.
Find out how many beads are in each group.
Take turns.

Try Use the corner of the red square.
Point to any number of beads on
the left side of the string.
Say that number.

Let your partner add 40 more
beads and point to the answer
with the blue square.

Start here

Say an addition
sentence that shows
what you and your
partner did.

Repeat until each partner gets 3 turns.

Try Again This time, add 50 more beads.
Talk about patterns you see when you add.

Center Activity ★ ★ 10-3

Play a Game

Share your thinking while you work.

Start Put ①②③④⑤ in a 🛍. Get 18 red squares.

Get a ⌇. Give one game board to each player. Play at the same time.

Try Place a ⌇ below one of these numbers.

25   **43**

Pick a tile. Put it here.

Add [ ] tens

Explain how to add that number of tens to the number you chose. Any player who has the sum covers it with a square. Put the tile back in the 🛍. Repeat until one player wins.

Four Corners

53	35	73
83	55	93
45	63	65

Four Corners

55	75	93
63	35	53
45	83	65

To win, be the first player to cover four corners.

Try Again Play again!

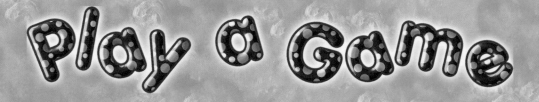

Share your thinking while you work.

Start  Put ⑴ ②③④⑤⑥ in a . Get 18 red squares.

Get a ⌐⌐⌐⌐⌐ . Give one game board to each player.
Play at the same time.

Try Place a ⌐⌐⌐⌐⌐ below one of these numbers.

14   **38**

Pick a tile. Put it here.

Add ☐ tens

Explain how to add that number of tens to the number
you chose. Any player who has the sum covers it with a square.
Put the tile back in the . Repeat until one player wins.

Four Corners

24	54	48
68	58	34
44	98	88

Four Corners

78	88	34
64	48	74
68	54	98

To win, be the first player to cover four corners.

Try Again Play again!

Play a Game

Partner Talk
Share your thinking while you work.

Start 🧒 Get a . Get 10 red squares.

Try Take turns. Point to **A** or **B**. Toss the 🎲. Cover the letter you chose with the 🎲. Look at the two-digit number, and the one-digit number on your 🎲. Tell how to add. Say the sum. If you regroup, take a red square.

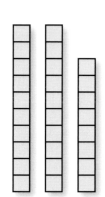

$$28 + \boxed{A} = \,?$$

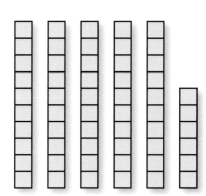

$$56 + \boxed{B} = \,?$$

Put your red squares here.

Player 1					
Player 2					

To win, collect 5 red squares.

Try Again Play again!

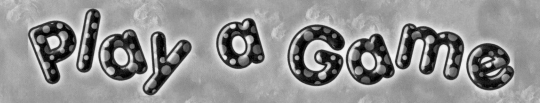

Share your thinking while you work.

Start 👥 Put 1 2 3 4 5 6 7 8 9 in a 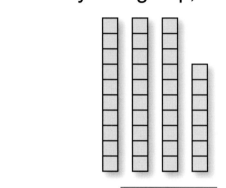.

Get 10 red squares.

Try Take turns. Point to **A** or **B**. Pick a number tile. Cover the letter you chose with your tile. Look at the two-digit number, and the one-digit number on your tile. Tell how to add. Say the sum. If you regroup, take a red square. Put the tile back in the 🛍️.

37 + | A | = ?   65 + | B | = ?

Put your red squares here.

| Player 1 | | | | | |
| Player 2 | | | | | |

To win, collect 5 red squares.

Try Again Play again!

Look and See

Partner Talk
Share your thinking while you work.

Start Put  0 1 2 3 4 5 6 in a .

Take turns until each partner gets 3 turns.

Try Choose a problem. Pick a number tile from the . Put the number tile in the empty space. Read the problem to your partner. Use the picture to help you solve the problem. Put the tile back in the .

Alina had 35 stamps.

She bought [ ] 0

more stamps.
How many stamps does Alina have now?

Logan has 39 toy cars.

Kevin gave Logan [ ] 0

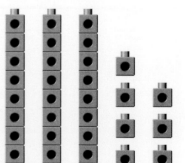

more toy cars.
How many toy cars does Logan have in all?

Try Again Play again! This time, say an addition sentence every time you add.

Look and See

Partner Talk

Share your thinking while you work.

Start  Get a and a .

Work together.

Try The farm store buys _____ seed packets of each kind.
Spin the spinner to find how many.

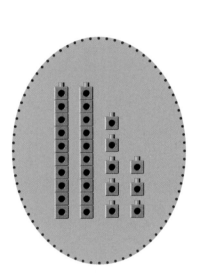

43	36
32	28

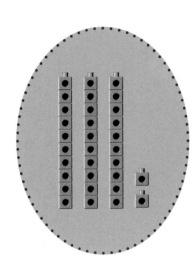

Find the picture that shows your number.
Answer the question below the chart.

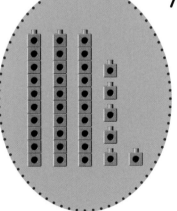

Seed Packets the Farm Store Already Has	
Pumpkin	20
Pepper	30
Corn	10
Tomato	40
Bean	50

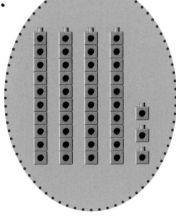

Question: How many packets of
each kind does the store have now?

Try Again Play again! This time, say an addition sentence
every time you add.

Partner Talk
Share your thinking while you work.

Start 👫 Get 12 red squares.
Cover each game space with a square.
Take turns.

Try Uncover two game spaces.

If you see two ways to subtract the same numbers, say the difference. Keep the squares.

If not, put the squares back where they were.

Take turns until all the spaces are uncovered.

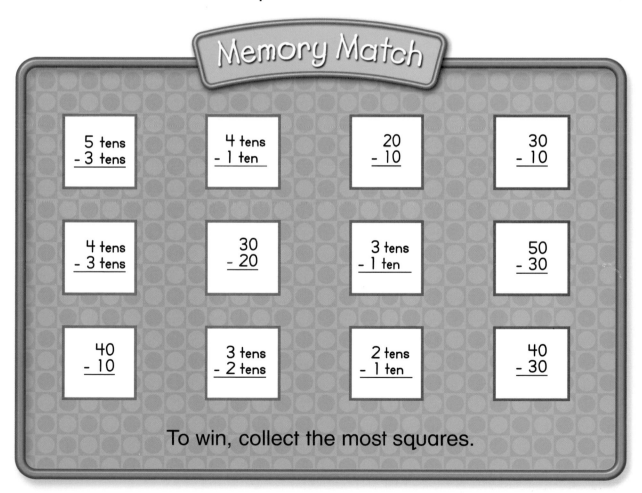

Memory Match

5 tens − 3 tens	4 tens − 1 ten	20 − 10	30 − 10
4 tens − 3 tens	30 − 20	3 tens − 1 ten	50 − 30
40 − 10	3 tens − 2 tens	2 tens − 1 ten	40 − 30

To win, collect the most squares.

Try Again Play again!

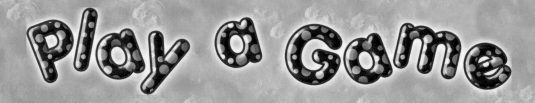

Partner Talk
Share your thinking while you work.

Start 🧍 Get 12 red squares.
Cover each game space with a square.
Take turns.

Try Uncover two game spaces.

If you see two ways to subtract the same numbers, say the difference. Keep the squares.

If not, put the squares back where they were.

Take turns until all the spaces are uncovered.

Memory Match

8 tens minus 3 tens	fifty minus forty	7 tens minus 4 tens	ninety minus fifty
seventy minus forty	8 tens minus 5 tens	9 tens minus 5 tens	6 tens minus 3 tens
eighty minus fifty	5 tens minus 4 tens	sixty minus thirty	eighty minus thirty

To win, collect the most squares.

Try Again Play again!

Partner Talk

Share your thinking while you work.

Start 👫 Take turns until each partner gets 5 turns.

Try Point to a baseball. Point to that number on the hundred chart. Let your partner point to a bat. Show how to subtract that number of tens from your number.

80   **50**

30   **40**

60   **70**

Subtract 30

Subtract 10

Subtract 20

1	2	3	4	5	6	7	8	9	10
11	12	13	14	15	16	17	18	19	20
21	22	23	24	25	26	27	28	29	30
31	32	33	34	35	36	37	38	39	40
41	42	43	44	45	46	47	48	49	50
51	52	53	54	55	56	57	58	59	60
61	62	63	64	65	66	67	68	69	70
71	72	73	74	75	76	77	78	79	80
81	82	83	84	85	86	87	88	89	90
91	92	93	94	95	96	97	98	99	100

Try Again This time, try to say the difference without looking at the chart.

Center Activity ★ **11-2**

Try Together

Partner Talk
Share your thinking while you work.

Start 👫 Take turns until each partner gets 5 turns.

Try Point to a number on a baseball.
Let your partner point to a bat. Count back to find the difference.
Look above the chart. Say that sentence with your numbers.

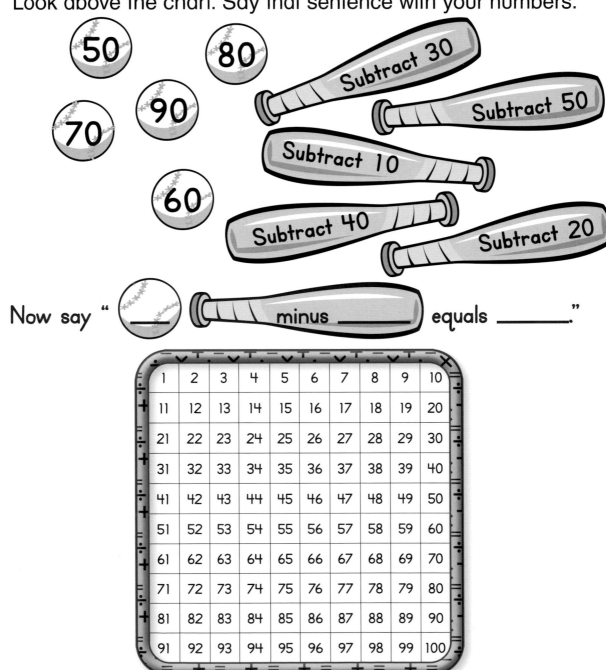

50   80

90
70

Subtract 30
Subtract 50
Subtract 10
60
Subtract 40   Subtract 20

Now say " ___ minus ___ equals ___ . "

1	2	3	4	5	6	7	8	9	10
11	12	13	14	15	16	17	18	19	20
21	22	23	24	25	26	27	28	29	30
31	32	33	34	35	36	37	38	39	40
41	42	43	44	45	46	47	48	49	50
51	52	53	54	55	56	57	58	59	60
61	62	63	64	65	66	67	68	69	70
71	72	73	74	75	76	77	78	79	80
81	82	83	84	85	86	87	88	89	90
91	92	93	94	95	96	97	98	99	100

Try Again This time, try to say the difference without looking at the chart.

Center Activity ★ ★ 11-2

Try Together

Start  Put ⌈1⌉ ⌈2⌉ ⌈3⌉ ⌈4⌉ ⌈5⌉ in a 🛍️.

Take turns until each of you gets 5 turns.

Try Point to 50, 60, 70, 80, or 90 on the chart. Pick a tile. Put that tile in the empty square. Ask your partner to subtract that two-digit number from the one you chose. Put the tile back in the 🛍️.

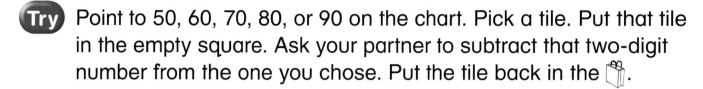

Subtract [ ] [0]

1	2	3	4	5	6	7	8	9	10
11	12	13	14	15	16	17	18	19	20
21	22	23	24	25	26	27	28	29	30
31	32	33	34	35	36	37	38	39	40
41	42	43	44	45	46	47	48	49	50
51	52	53	54	55	56	57	58	59	60
61	62	63	64	65	66	67	68	69	70
71	72	73	74	75	76	77	78	79	80
81	82	83	84	85	86	87	88	89	90
91	92	93	94	95	96	97	98	99	100

Try Again Talk about why the tens digit changes and the ones digit stays the same when you subtract 10, 20, 30, 40, or 50.

Center Activity ★ 11-3

Try Together

Partner Talk

Share your thinking while you work.

Start 👫 Get ⬚1 ⬚2 ⬚3 ⬚4 ⬚5 ⬚6 ⬚7 ⬚8 ⬚9.

Take turns until each of you gets 5 turns.

Try Point to 50, 60, 70, 80, or 90 on the chart. Point to a number above it in the same column. Ask your partner to say the difference. Place a number tile in the square below to show that difference.

1	2	3	4	5	6	7	8	9	10
11	12	13	14	15	16	17	18	19	20
21	22	23	24	25	26	27	28	29	30
31	32	33	34	35	36	37	38	39	40
41	42	43	44	45	46	47	48	49	50
51	52	53	54	55	56	57	58	59	60
61	62	63	64	65	66	67	68	69	70
71	72	73	74	75	76	77	78	79	80
81	82	83	84	85	86	87	88	89	90
91	92	93	94	95	96	97	98	99	100

The difference is | 0 .

Try Again Pick a tile. Show a difference. Ask your partner to point to two numbers you can subtract to get that difference.

Center Activity ★ ★ 11-3

Cover Three

Share your thinking while you work.

Start 👥 Get . Get 6 red squares. Get 6 blue squares. Take turns.

Try Pick a number in a circle. Toss .
Subtract that many tens. Say the difference.

If you see the difference on the game board,
cover it with a square.

If not, lose your turn.

(80) 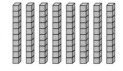   (70)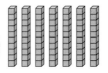

40	70	60
30	10	60
40	20	50

To win, get: ■■■ or ■ or ■ or ■

Try Again Talk about how you subtract tens.
Use the place-value blocks to explain what you do.

Cover Three

Start Put ❶ ❷ ❸ ❹ ❺ ❻ ❼ ❽ ❾ in a 🛍️.

Try Pick a number. Say the difference next to that number. Can you find a subtraction problem on the game board that goes with the number? If yes, cover it with a square. If no, lose your turn. Put the number back in the 🛍️.

70 - 40	80 - 10	80 - 60
50 - 20	30 - 20	50 - 30
80 - 20	70 - 30	60 - 20

❶	The difference is 40
❷	The difference is 20
❸	The difference is 30
❹	The difference is 70
❺	The difference is 20
❻	The difference is 60
❼	The difference is 30
❽	The difference is 40
❾	The difference is 10

To win, get: ■ ■ ■ or ■ or ■ or ■
               ■   ■   ■
               ■   ■   ■

Try Again Tell a subtraction story using the numbers in each space on the game board.

Look and See

Start 🏃 Put   in a 🛍️.
Take turns until each partner gets 3 turns.

Try Choose a problem. Pick a number tile from the 🛍️.
Put the number tile in the empty space. Read the problem
to your partner. Use the picture to help you solve the problem.
Put the tile back in the 🛍️.

A store has 60 paper cups.

It sells [ ]0

of those paper cups.
How many paper cups does the store have left?

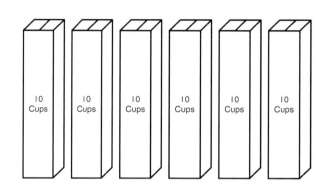

Joseph and Ellen have 80 marbles in all.

Joseph has [ ]0

marbles.
How many marbles does Ellen have?

Try Again Play again! This time, say a subtraction sentence
every time you subtract.

Look and See

Start 👥 Get a ✏️ and a 📎 .
Work together.

Try The farm store needs _____ seed packets of each kind.
Spin the spinner to find how many.

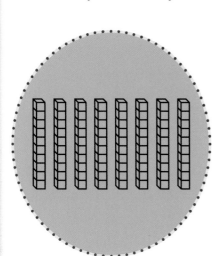

90	60
80	70

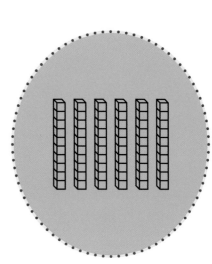

**Find the picture that shows your number.
Answer the question below the chart.**

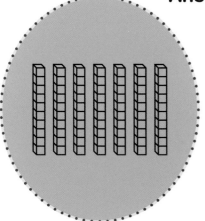

Seed Packets the Farm Store has Now	
Pumpkin	40
Pepper	50
Corn	20
Tomato	30
Bean	10

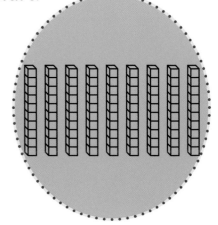

**Question: How many more packets of
each kind should the store get?**

Try Again Play again! This time, say a subtraction sentence
every time you subtract.

Center Activity ⭐⭐ 11-5

Look and See

Start 大 Get  .

Get 2 red squares. Work together.

Try Look at each row of objects.
Put the objects in order from shortest to longest.

Put ⬜**1** below the shortest one. Put ⬜**3** below the longest one.

Put ⬜**2** below the other one.

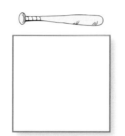

Now use the corner of a square to point to each answer.
Are the balls in order?   Are the caps in order?

yes ◇   no ◇   yes ◇   no ◇

Try Again Find two books. Tell which one is taller.
Tell which one is shorter.

Look and See

Partner Talk
Share your thinking while you work.

Start 👥 Get  1 2 3 . Get ✏ ✏ .

Get 2 red squares. Work together.

Try Look at one group of objects. Put the objects in order from shortest to longest.

Put 1 near the shortest one. Put 3 near the longest one.

Put 2 near the other one. Remove the tiles. Try a different group.

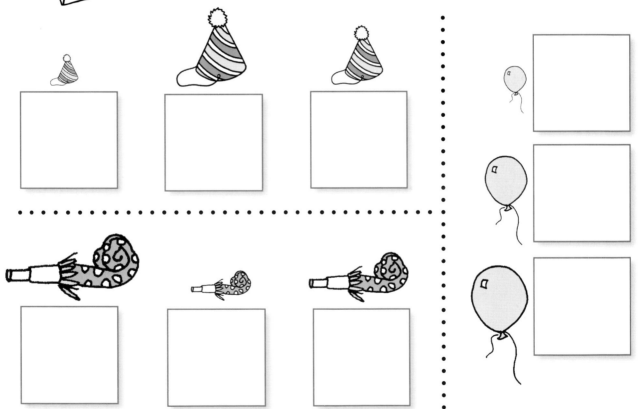

Now look at the next sets of objects. Put a paper clip below the longest one. Put a square below the shortest one.

Try Again Order the lengths of three of your fingers.

Helping Hands

Partner Talk

Share your thinking while you work.

 **Start** 👫 Put  in a 🛍 .

Get 10 red squares.

Try Pick a number tile to find a piece of yarn.
Line up squares along your piece of yarn to measure it. Your partner
picks a number tile and puts it next to that piece of yarn.
Move your red squares to your partner's piece of yarn. Tell which
piece of yarn is longer. Repeat until each player gets 5 turns.

1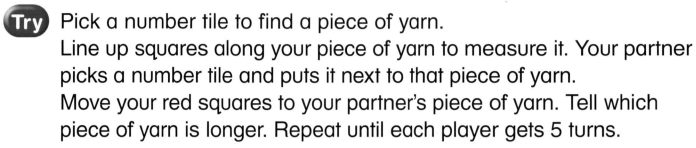

2

3

4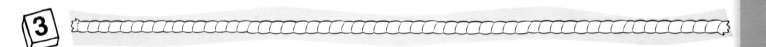

5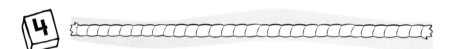

6

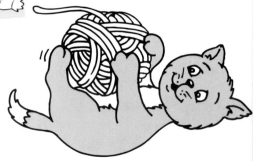

Try Again Play again.

Helping Hands

Partner Talk

Share your thinking while you work.

Start  Put [1] [2] [3] [4] [5] [6] in a 🛍 .

Get 10 red squares.

Try Pick a number tile and put it next to that piece of cheese. Work together. Line up squares along your piece of cheese to measure it. Then move your squares above another piece of cheese. Tell if that piece of cheese is longer or shorter than the first piece of cheese you measured. Keep moving your squares to compare with all other pieces of cheese. Play until the bag is empty.

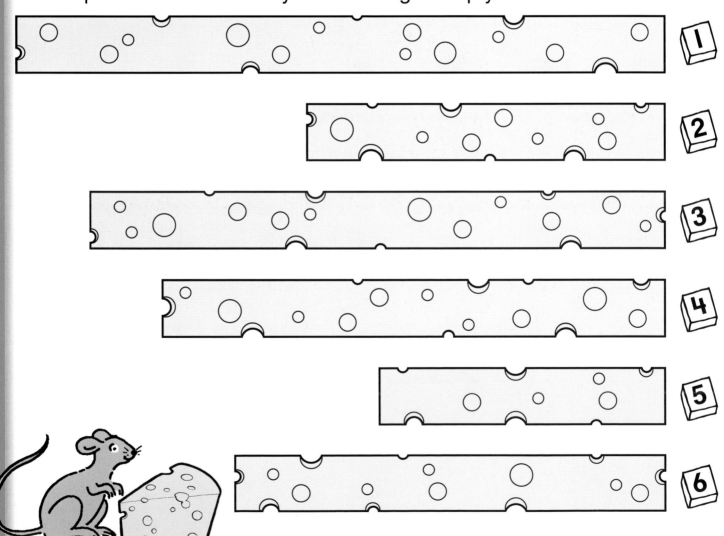

Try Again Play again.

Try Together

Start 🏃 Get 10 red squares. Work together.

Try Choose an object.
Estimate how many sides of squares you need to measure it.
Put sides of squares end-to-end to measure your object.
Compare your estimate to your measurement.

Try Again Find and measure one or more pencils.

Try Together

Start 👥 Get 9 red squares. Work together.

Try Line up the sides of your squares end-to-end in the rectangle. Choose a flower. Estimate the length of that flower and its stem. Use the sides of your squares to measure it. Put the squares back in the rectangle. Try every flower.

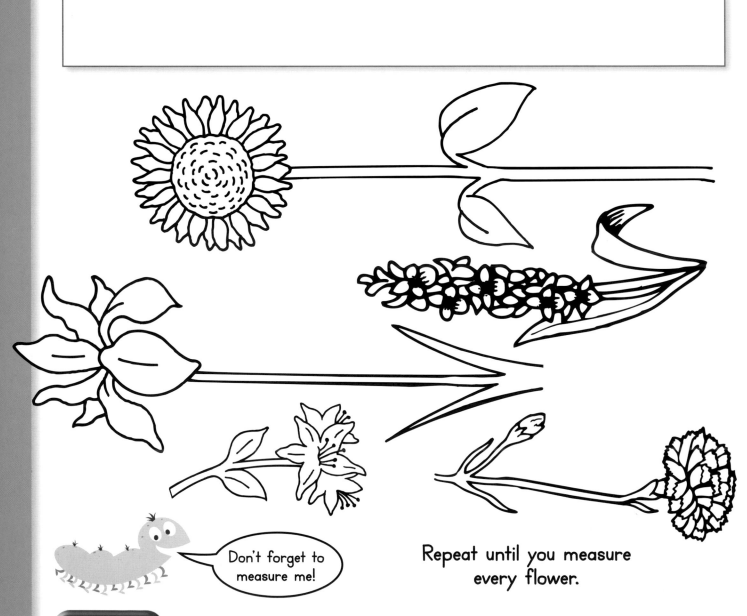

Don't forget to measure me!

Repeat until you measure every flower.

Try Again This time, estimate and measure the leaves and the caterpillar.

Look and See

Partner Talk
Share your thinking while you work.

Start 👫 Get 11 red squares. Get 11 blue squares.
Take turns until each partner gets 5 turns.

Try Find 3 balls that have different paths.
Measure the path of each ball with sides of squares.
Order the paths from shortest to longest.

1

2

3

9

6

4

5

7

8

Try Again Find three objects in your classroom.
Order them from shortest to tallest.

Center Activity ★ 12-4

Look and See

Start 👥 Get 11 red squares. Get 11 blue squares.
Take turns until each partner gets 4 turns.

Try Find 3 different paths that the snails made. Use sides of squares to measure each path. Order the paths from longest to shortest.

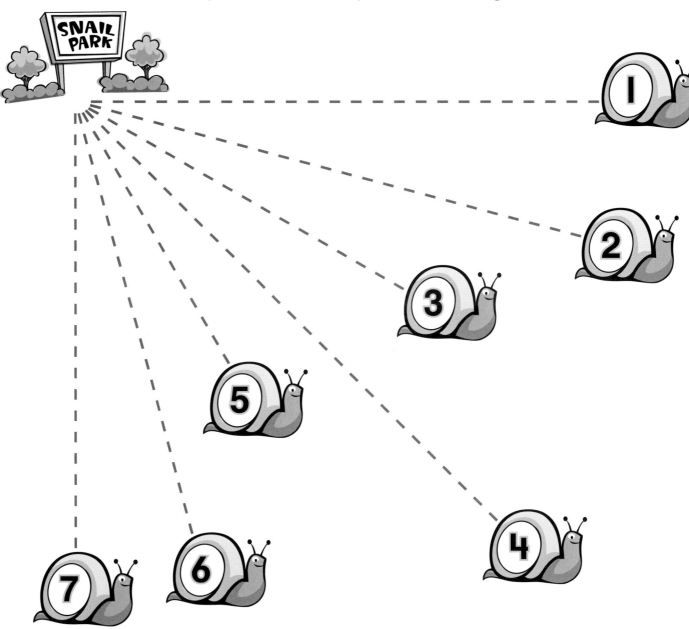

Try Again Find three objects in your classroom.
Order them from tallest to shortest.

Helping Hands

Partner Talk — Share your thinking while you work.

Start 🏃 Get ① ② ③ ④ ⑤ ⑥ ⑦ ⑧ ⑨ and
① ② ③ ④ ⑤ ⑥ ⑦ ⑧ ⑨ .

Get 6 red squares. Get ⬭ ⬭ ⬭ ⬭ .

Try Measure each other's fingers. Use ⬭ . Then use squares.
Use a tile to show each measurement.

Player 1		Player 2	
about	about	about	about
paper clips	squares	paper clips	squares
paper clips	squares	paper clips	squares
paper clips	squares	paper clips	squares
paper clips	squares	paper clips	squares

Try Again Measure the fruit with squares. Then use your thumb
to measure. Why do you get different answers?

Helping Hands

Partner Talk
Share your thinking while you work.

Start 👥 Get  and

1 2 3 4 5 6 7 8 9 .

Get 6 red squares. Get ⌐⌐ ⌐⌐ ⌐⌐ ⌐⌐ .

Try Choose a line. About how many sides of squares will it take to measure it? Use a tile to show your estimate. Measure to check. Who made the closer estimate?

Player 1   Player 2

_____

_____

_____

_____

_____

Now go back. Estimate and
measure again using paper clips.

Try Again Talk about reasons why we do not use squares and paper clips together to measure an object.

Center Activity ☆ ☆ **12-5**

Try Together

Partner Talk

Share your thinking while you work.

Start 🏃 Get 14 red squares. Cover every circle with a red square.

Get ⓪ ① ② ③ ④ ⑤ ⑥ ⑦ . Work together.

Try Uncover a circle. Say the name of the object.
Tell whether you would measure it in cubes or straws.

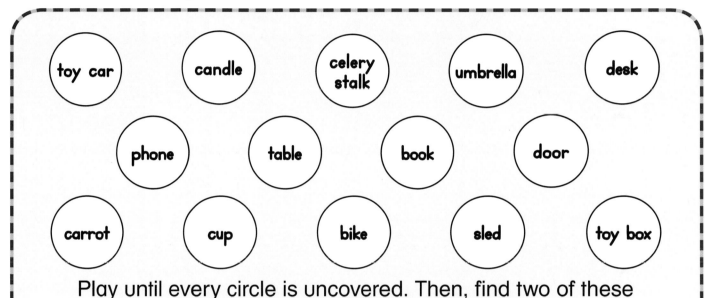

(toy car) (candle) (celery stalk) (umbrella) (desk)

(phone) (table) (book) (door)

(carrot) (cup) (bike) (sled) (toy box)

Play until every circle is uncovered. Then, find two of these
objects that are about the same length.

Point to an item below. Estimate its length in number tiles.
Measure it by using number tiles end-to-end. Say the length.

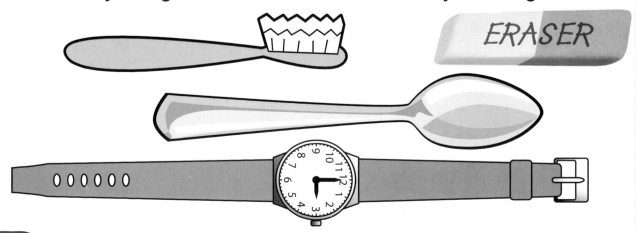

ERASER

Try Again Find another object. Estimate and measure its length.

Try Together

Partner Talk

Share your thinking while you work.

Start  Get ⓪ ⓪ ① ① ② ③ ④ ⑤ ⑥ ⑦ ⑧ ⑨.

Work together.

Try Read each problem. Share your ideas.

a. You want to measure your classroom door. A classmate says to measure it in cubes. Do you agree?

b. You tell your friend that your pencil is 6 cubes long. Hold your two thumbs apart to show the length of your pencil between your thumbs.

c. You tell your friend that your kitten is ten cubes long. Hold your hands apart to show the length of the kitten between your two hands.

d. Your lunchbox has the length of about one straw. Your friend says his 4-straw-long toy horn fits in your lunchbox. Tell if you agree.

e. Would you measure the length of your table in cubes or straws? Explain.

f. You want to know the length of your jump rope. Is it easier to measure it in cubes or straws? Tell why.

Use number tiles to measure the length of each object:

a crayon

your thumb

your eraser

a pencil

your partner's hand

the length of this paper

Try Again This time, find something else to measure using number tiles. Tell when you think it is easier to measure in straws instead of number tiles.

Look and See

Start 🏃 Put 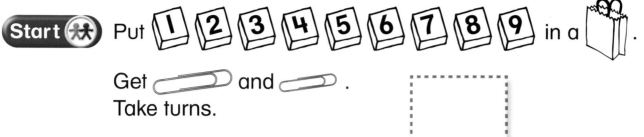 1 2 3 4 5 6 7 8 9 in a 🛍.

Get ⊂⊃ and ⊂⊃ .
Take turns.

Try Pick a tile. Put your tile here. ➡️ ⬜ o'clock

Use paper clips. Show that time on your clock.
Ask your partner to say the time. Repeat until the 🛍 is empty.

Try Again Put the tiles back in the 🛍. Repeat the activity.
This time, tell what you do at that hour.

Look and See

Start 🏃 Get one . Get ⬭ and ⬭.
Take turns until each partner gets 5 turns.

Try Toss the 🎲. Follow directions. Use paper clips.
Show the time on the clock. Ask your partner to say the time.

⚀	Show 7 o'clock.	⚄	Show 12 o'clock.
⚁	Show 11 o'clock.	⚂	Show 9 o'clock.
⚃	Show 4 o'clock.	⚅	Pick a time. Tell why you like it.

Try Again Repeat the activity. This time, tell what you do at that hour during the day and at night.

Helping Hands

Partner Talk

Share your thinking while you work.

Start 🚶 Get ⊂═══⊃ and ⊂═══⊃ .
Take turns.

Try Point to a digital clock. Ask your partner to say that time.
Use paper clips to put hands on the clock. Show that time.

Try Again Tell what you might be doing at each hour.

Helping Hands

Start Get

Get ⬭ and ⬭. Take turns.

Try Point to a balloon. Say the time together.
Show that time on both clocks.

Try Again Show other times that you know on the clocks.
Say those times.

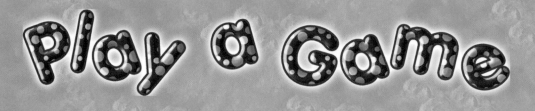

Partner Talk

Share your thinking while you work.

Start 👫 Get 12 red squares.
Cover each game space with a square. Take turns.

Try Uncover two game spaces.

If you see two times that are the same, say those times. Keep the squares.

If not, put the squares back where they were.

Take turns until all the spaces are uncovered.

Memory Match

1:30	twelve o'clock	half past nine	eight thirty
12:00	8:30	3:00	seven o'clock
three o'clock	half past one	7:00	9:30

To win, collect the most squares.

Try Again Play again!

Play a Game

Partner Talk

Share your thinking while you work.

Start 大 Get 12 red squares.
Cover each game space with a square. Take turns.

Try Uncover two game spaces.

If you match a time with another time that is 30 minutes later, say the time that is 30 minutes later in two different ways. Keep the squares.

If not, put the squares back where they were.

Take turns until all the spaces are uncovered.

Memory Match

11:00	3:30	9:30	5:00
5:30	1:30	9:00	11:30
7:00	3:00	7:30	1:00

To win, collect the most squares.

Try Again Play again!

 1

Listen and Learn

Partner Talk
Share your thinking while you work.

Start 👥 Take turns. Read the name of a schedule.
How many times are in that schedule?

Try Ask your partner a question.
For example, ask: At what time is the last animal show?
Take turns until each player answers 5 or more questions.

Zoo Feeding Schedule	
Elephants	7:30
Giraffes	8:00
Zebras	9:00
Monkeys	9:30
Dolphins	10:00
Gorillas	10:30
Camels	11:30
Wolves	12:00

Bus Schedule	
To the Zoo	From the Zoo
8:00	9:30
10:00	10:30
1:00	1:30
3:00	3:30
5:00	5:30

Train Schedule	
To the Zoo	From the Zoo
7:30	8:00
8:30	9:00
11:30	1:00
3:30	4:00
4:30	5:00

Animal Show Schedule	
Dolphin Show	11:00
Bird Show	1:00
Petting Zoo	2:00
Seal Show	3:00

Try Again This time, say a time in one of the schedules.
Ask your partner to tell what happens at that time.

Listen and Learn

Partner Talk
Share your thinking while you work.

Start 👥 Get 📝.

Try You and your partner are going to the zoo. Look at the schedules. Plan your day. How are you going to get to the zoo? What are you going to do at the zoo? How will you get home? Make a schedule for your day.

Zoo Feeding Schedule	
Elephants	7:30
Giraffes	8:00
Zebras	9:00
Monkeys	9:30
Dolphins	10:00
Gorillas	10:30
Camels	11:30
Wolves	12:00

Bus Schedule	
To the Zoo	From the Zoo
8:00	9:30
10:00	10:30
1:00	1:30
3:00	3:30
5:00	5:30

Train Schedule	
To the Zoo	From the Zoo
7:30	8:00
8:30	9:00
11:30	1:00
3:30	4:00
4:30	5:00

Animal Show Schedule	
Dolphin Show	11:00
Bird Show	1:00
Petting Zoo	2:00
Seal Show	3:00

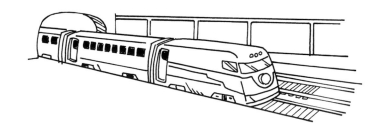

Try Again Make a schedule for a different day at the zoo.

Helping Hands

Partner Talk

Share your thinking while you work.

Start 👥 Put 8 red squares and 8 blue squares in a . Work together.

Try Take some squares out of the 🛍. Separate them by color on the workmat. Put them on the graph. Answer the questions.
When you finish, put the squares in the 🛍. Make 6 or more graphs.

Red Squares	Workmat	Blue Squares

Red Squares								
Blue Squares								

QUESTIONS

1. Do you have the same number of squares for each color?
2. Does each square have a partner?
3. How many more red squares are there than blue squares?

OR

How many more blue squares are there than red squares?

Try Again Make more graphs! Tell why it is easier to see which row has more if the squares are in pairs.

Helping Hands

Partner Talk
Share your thinking while you work.

Start 👥 Put [4] [4] [5] [5] [6] [6] [7] [7] in a 🛍.

Put [1] [2] [3] in a another 🛍.

Get a 📎.

Get 10 red squares for one player.

Get 10 blue squares for the other player.

Red Squares	Blue Squares

Try

STEP 1 Each player picks a tile from the 🛍 with 4 – 7. Put that number of your squares on the graph.

STEP 2 Read and answer these questions:
   a. Does each square have a partner?
   b. How many more red squares are there than blue squares?
                    OR
   How many more blue squares are there than red squares?

STEP 3 Choose either + or – . Put a 📎 below it. Ask your partner to pick a tile from the 🛍 with 1 – 3. Add or subtract that number of squares from your partner's squares on the graph. Answer the questions in STEP 2 again.

   ✛   ➖

Try Again Make more graphs! Tell why it is easier to compare two groups of squares if you make a graph.

Look and See

Start Get 12 red squares. Work together.

Try First graders made this picture graph.
Talk about the number of favorite toys of each kind.
Answer each question below the graph.
Use squares to cover the answers you do not choose.

First Graders' Favorite Toys								
Truck	🚚	🚚	🚚	🚚	🚚			
Bear	🧸	🧸	🧸	🧸	🧸	🧸		
Doll	🎎	🎎	🎎					

1. What is the graph about?

Toys	Colors	Books

2. Which toy was chosen most by the children?

Truck	Bear	Doll

3. How many more children like bears than dolls?

3	2	4

4. How many children named their favorite toy to make this graph?

12	11	14

5. Which of these three toys is your favorite?

Truck	Bear	Doll

6. Which of these three toys is your partner's favorite?

Truck	Bear	Doll

How would your choices change the graph?

Try Again Take turns. Ask another question about the graph.
Ask your partner to answer your question.

Look and See

Start Get 8 red squares.
Work together.

Try The graph shows the number of different trees in a park. Talk about the number of trees of each kind. Answer each question below the graph. Use squares to cover the answers you do not choose.

Trees Growing in Carver Park							
Maple	🍁	🍁	🍁	🍁	🍁	🍁	
🍂 Oak	🍂	🍂					
🍃 Elm	🍃	🍃	🍃	🍃			

1. Which row shows the most trees growing in the park?

   | Maple | Oak | Elm |

2. Which row shows the fewest trees growing in the park?

   | Maple | Oak | Elm |

3. How many more maple trees than elm trees grow in the park?

   | 3 | 2 | 7 |

4. Is this graph helpful if you want to know how many children are playing in the park?

   | Yes | No |

5. What if the city removed an elm tree? Would you have to change any answer in question 1, 2, or 3?

6. What if the city planted one more oak tree? Take a square. Add it to the graph to show the extra tree. Answer the questions again.

Try Again Take turns. Ask another question about the graph.
Ask your partner to answer your question.

Try Together

Partner Talk

Share your thinking while you work.

Start 👤 Get 11 red squares. Work together.

Try Look at the bar graph that first graders made.
Talk about the number of children who chose each activity.

Favorite Activities							
🚲 Bike Riding							
🛼 Skating							
🪢 Jumping Rope							
	0	1	2	3	4	5	6	7

Number of Children

Answer each question about the graph.
Use squares to cover the answers you do not choose.

1. What is the graph about?

| Activities | Food | Clothes |

2. How many children like skating best?

| 5 | 4 | 3 |

3. How many more children like bike riding than skating?

| 5 | 2 | 3 |

4. How many children like bike riding and jumping rope?

| 9 | 6 | 4 |

5. Did 13 children vote for a favorite activity? Why or why not?

| Yes | No |

Try Again Put squares on the graph to show your favorite activity and your partner's favorite activity. Take turns asking and answering questions about the new graph.

Try Together

Partner Talk

Share your thinking while you work.

Start Get 9 red squares. Work together.

Try Look at the bar graph.
Talk about the number of books sold on each day.

Books Sold at the Bargain Book Store													
Monday													
Tuesday													
Wednesday													
Thursday													
Friday													

0   1   2   3   4   5   6   7   8   9   10   11   12   13
Number of Books

Answer each question about the graph.
Use squares to cover the answers you do not choose.

1. What is the graph about?

| Roses | Books | Toys |

2. How many books were sold on Wednesday?

| 6 | 9 | 8 |

3. How many more books were sold on Tuesday than on Monday?

| 3 | 4 | 2 |

4. What is the greatest number of books sold on one day?

| 8 | 9 | 10 |

5. Did the store ever sell more than 10 books in one day?

| Yes | No |

Try Again Take turns. On your turn, ask another question about the graph. Ask your partner to answer your question.

Look and See

Partner Talk
Share your thinking while you work.

Start 🏃 Get 1 2 3 4 5 6 7 8 9 .

Get 16 red squares. Work together.

Try Look at the toy cars. Organize them by color.
Use squares to show tally marks.
When you have a group of five, pile them up.
Then use number tiles to show your totals.

	Tally Marks	Total
White Cars		
Black Cars		
Grey Cars		

1. Which group has the most cars?

2. Which group has the least?

3. Which group has two fewer than another group?

Try Again Take turns. Ask and answer other questions
about the data in the chart.

Center Activity ★ 14-4

Look and See

Partner Talk

Share your thinking while you work.

Start 🏃 Get 0 1 2 3 4 5 6 7 8 9

and 0 1 2 3 4 5 6 7 8 9 .

Get 24 squares. Work together.

Try Look at the figures. Organize them by shape.

a	Triangle
b	Square
c	Circle

Use squares to show tally marks. When you have a group of five, pile them up. Then use number tiles to show your totals.

	Tally Marks	Total	
a			
b			
c			

QUESTIONS

1. Which group has the most?
2. Which group has the least?

Next, organize the figures by color. Then answer the questions again.

a	Light grey
b	Dark grey
c	White

Finally, organize the figures by size. Then answer the questions again.

a	Small
b	Medium
c	Large

Try Again This time, ask and answer other questions about the data in the chart.

Helping Hands

Partner Talk
Share your thinking while you work.

Start  Get ⎡1⎤ ⎡2⎤ ⎡3⎤ ⎡4⎤ ⎡5⎤ .

Get 🎲 🎲 🎲 🎲 . Get 5 red squares. Get 5 blue squares. Get a 🛍. Work together.

Try Put some cubes, some red squares, some blue squares, and some number tiles in the 🛍. Spill them out. Organize the objects on the real-object graph. Answer the questions below the graph.

🎲					
Red Squares					
Blue Squares					
Number Tiles					

QUESTIONS

1. Which group has the greatest number of things?
2. Suppose you added two more number cubes. How many would there be on the graph?
3. How many red squares and blue squares are there in all?
4. Which group has the least number of things?

Try Again Play again. This time put different numbers of things in the 🛍.

Helping Hands

Partner Talk
Share your thinking while you work.

Start Get 8 red squares. Get 8 blue squares.

Put **1 2 3 4 5 6 7** in a bag. Work together.

Try Pick a tile. Find that design. R means red. B means blue. Talk about how many red squares and blue squares you would need to make it. Put squares on the graph to show the number of squares of each color.

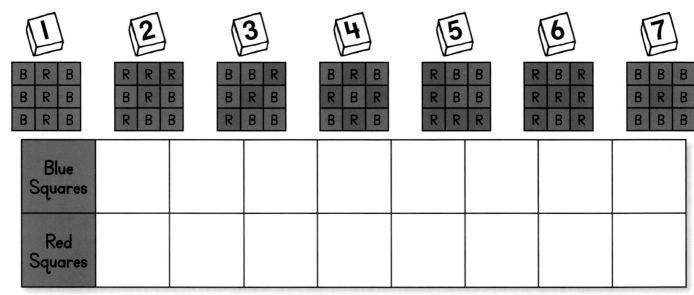

	1	2	3	4	5	6	7
	B R B	R R R	B B R	B R B	R B B	R B R	B B B
	B R B	B R B	B R B	R B R	R B B	R R R	B R B
	B R B	R B B	R B B	B R B	R R R	R B R	B B B

Blue Squares							
Red Squares							

Now, take the squares from the graph. Place them below.
Make the design you chose.

SUPPOSE YOU WANT TO MAKE TWO OF THE DESIGNS. HOW MANY SQUARES OF EACH COLOR DO YOU NEED?

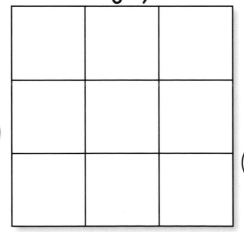

IF YOU WANT TO MAKE THE WORD "HI," HOW MANY SQUARES OF EACH COLOR DO YOU NEED?

Try Again Set the tile aside. Remove the squares.
Repeat until the bag of tiles is empty.

Helping Hands

 Partner Talk

Share your thinking while you work.

Start 👫 Work together.

Try Some first graders took a survey of their favorite stickers. The first tally chart shows their data. Use your finger to trace each of the shapes on the picture graph. In which row did you trace a picture in every space?

Favorite Stickers		
a	⭐	||||
b	💜	卌 |
c	✳	|||

Favorite Erasers		
a	▭	卌
b	▲	卌 |
c	⬭	||

Now look at the tally chart of the first graders' favorite erasers.
Use your finger to trace the eraser shapes on the graph.
In which row did you have one extra space?

a						
b						
c						

Try Again Take turns. Ask a **how many more** or **how many fewer** question about the data in one of the tally charts. Ask your partner to answer your question.

Center Activity ⭐ 14-6

Helping Hands

Partner Talk
Share your thinking while you work.

Start 👫 Get ⬜1 ⬜2 ⬜3 ⬜4 ⬜5 ⬜6 .
Get 4 red squares. Work together.

Try Jill took a survey of the toys in her toy box. Look at her tally chart. Put a number tile in each row to show the number in all. Answer the two questions. Use squares to cover the answers you do not choose.

Block	‖‖	
Marble	‖‖‖ ‖	
Ring	‖‖‖	

QUESTIONS
1. Which group has the most?

| Blocks | Marbles | Rings |

2. Which group has the least number?

| Blocks | Marbles | Rings |

Then trace each toy with your finger on the graph.

Block						
Marble						
Ring						

If you added 2 more rings, would that group have the most?

Try Again Take turns. Make up another question.
Ask your partner to answer it.

Helping Hands

Start 👫 Get 20 red squares. Work together.

Try Look at the tally chart. Use squares to make a bar graph. Then read each question. Point to the answer.

KINDS OF FRUIT IN THE BAG	
Apples	~~||||~~ |||
Bananas	~~||||~~	
Oranges	|||
Pears	|||

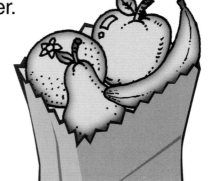

DIFFERENT KINDS OF FRUIT IN THE BAG								
Apples								
Bananas								
Oranges								
Pears								

0   1   2   3   4   5   6   7   8

1. The bag has the most of which fruit?

      Apples   Bananas   Pears

2. How many more bananas are there than pears?

      3 more   4 more   6 more

3. How many oranges and apples are there in all?

      10 in all   11 in all   12 in all

Try Again Take turns. Make up a question about the graph. Ask your partner to answer it.

Center Activity ★ 14-7

Helping Hands

Start 🚶 Get  0 1 2 3 4 5 6 7 8 9 .

Get 20 red squares.
Work together.

Try Use the tally chart to make a bar graph.

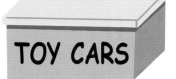
TOY CARS

COLORS OF CARS IN THE BOX	
Red Cars	IIII I
Blue Cars	IIII III
Green Cars	IIII
Orange Cars	II

DIFFERENT COLORS OF CARS IN THE BOX

	0	1	2	3	4	5	6	7	8
Red									
Blue									
Green									
Orange									

1. How many more blue cars are there than red cars?

2. How many blue cars and red cars are there in all?

3. How many red cars and green cars are there in all?

4. How many more red cars are there than orange cars?

Answer each question with a number sentence. Use number tiles.

+ or **−** **=**

Try Again Take turns. Make up a question about the graph.
Ask your partner to answer it.

Cover Three

Start 👥 Put   in a 🛍️.

Get 6 red squares. Get 6 blue squares. Take turns.

Try Pick a tile. Follow the directions.
Cover that shape. Put your tile back in the 🛍️.

1	Cover a circle.
2	Cover a triangle.
3	Cover a rectangle.

To win, get: ■■■ or ■ or ■ or ■.

Try Again Remove your squares. Play again!

 Cover Three

 Partner Talk
Share your thinking while you work.

Start Put 0 3 4 in a .

Get 6 red squares.
Get 6 blue squares. Take turns.

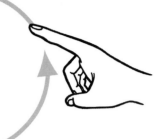

Try Pick a tile.

Trace in the air: • A shape with that number of straight sides
  • The letters in the name of that shape

Cover the name of the shape. Put your tile back in the 🛍.

Rectangle	Triangle	Circle
Square	Rectangle	Square
Triangle	Circle	Triangle

To win, get: ■ ■ ■ or ■ or ■   or   ■.
                    ■   ■   ■
                    ■   ■   ■

Try Again Remove your squares. Play again!

Helping Hands

Start Put 0 1 2 3 4 5 6 in a bag.

Get 7 red squares.
Get 6 blue squares.
Take turns.

Try Pick a tile. Put that number of blue squares on the giraffe. Ask your partner to fill the other spaces with red squares. Put your tile where it belongs in the list. Remove the squares. Take turns until you finish the list.

Red	Blue
1	
2	
3	
4	
5	
6	
7	

Try Again Now that your list is organized, take turns. Say the ways you found to fill the giraffe with 7 squares. Play again!

Center Activity 15-2

Partner Talk — Share your thinking while you work.

Center Activity 15-2

Copyright © Pearson Education, Inc., or its affiliates. All Rights Reserved. 1

Helping Hands

Partner Talk
Share your thinking while you work.

Start 👫 Put  in a 🛍️.

Get 9 red squares. Get 9 blue squares. Take turns.

Try Pick a tile. Put that number of blue squares on the elephant.
Ask your partner to fill the other spaces with red squares.
Put your tile where it belongs in one of the lists.
Remove the squares. Take turns until you finish both lists.

Red	Blue		Red	Blue
0			5	
1			6	
2			7	
3			8	
4			9	

Try Again Now that your lists are organized, take turns. Say the ways you found to fill the elephant with 9 squares. Play again!

Play a Game

Partner Talk Share your thinking while you work.

Start 🚶 Get 12 red squares.
Cover each game space with a square. Take turns.

Try Uncover two game spaces.

If the two shapes have the same number of corners, explain why. Keep the squares.

If not, put the squares back where they were.

Take turns until all the spaces are uncovered.

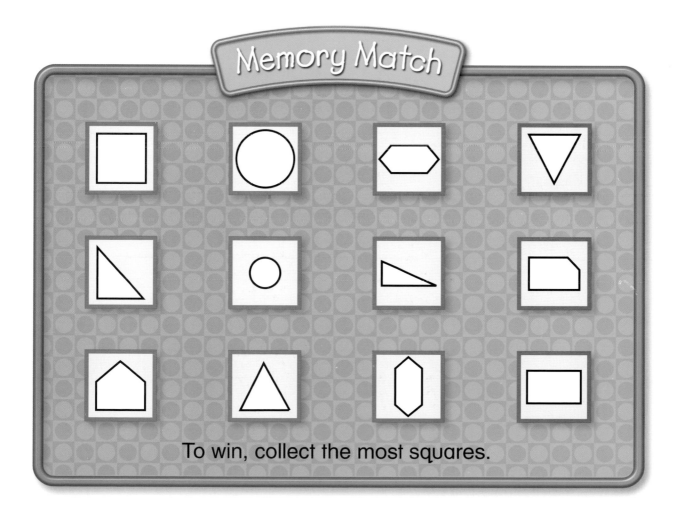

Memory Match

To win, collect the most squares.

Try Again Play again!

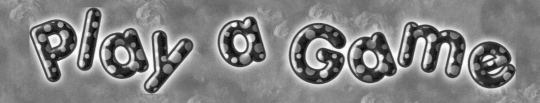 Play a Game

Partner Talk
Share your thinking while you work.

Start 👫 Get 12 red squares.
Cover each game space with a square. Take turns.

Try Uncover two game spaces. Do you see one shape and a way to describe that shape?

If you do, name the shape and read the words. Keep the squares.

If not, put the squares back where they were.

Take turns until all the spaces are uncovered.

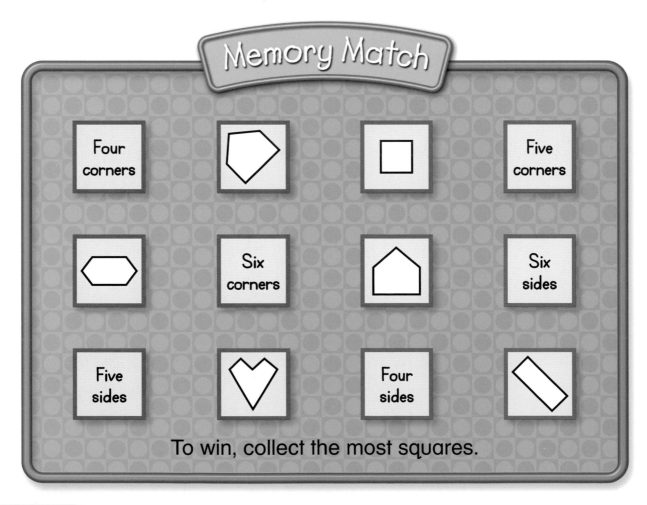

Memory Match

Four corners	⬠	◻	Five corners
⬡	Six corners	⬠	Six sides
Five sides	♡	Four sides	▱

To win, collect the most squares.

Try Again Play again!

Math in Motion

Partner Talk
Share your thinking while you work.

Start 👥 Put  0 1 2 3 4 5 6 7 8 9 in a 🛍. Take turns.

Try Pick a tile from the 🛍 to find your puzzle. Use your finger to trace all its shapes. Find your missing puzzle piece. Point to it. Use your finger to trace it. Cover it with your tile. Take turns until the 🛍 is empty.

PUZZLES

This piece is missing.

PUZZLE PIECES

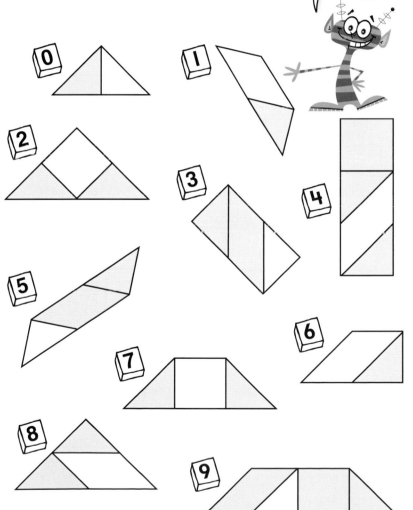

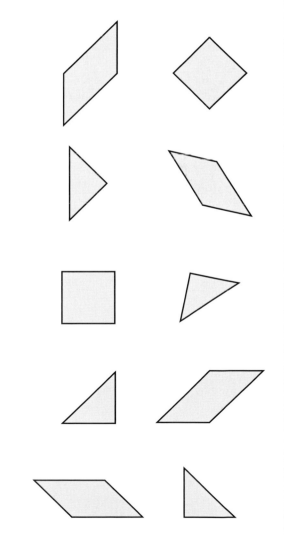

Try Again Put the tiles back in the 🛍. Play again!

Math in Motion

Partner Talk
Share your thinking while you work.

Start 👥 Put ⬚1 ⬚2 ⬚3 ⬚4 ⬚5 ⬚6 in a 🛍.
Get 12 red squares. Take turns.

Try Pick a tile from the 🛍 to find your puzzle. Use your finger to trace all its shapes. Find your two missing puzzle pieces. Put red squares on both pieces. Set the tile aside. Take turns until the 🛍 is empty.

These two pieces are missing.

PUZZLES

PUZZLE PIECES

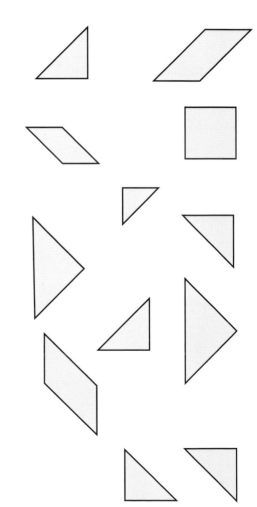

Try Again Put the tiles back in the 🛍. Play again!

Helping Hands

Partner Talk — Share your thinking while you work.

Start  Put 2 3 4 5 6 7 8 9 in a 🛍.

Get these pattern blocks:

2 ⬡ , 4 ⬯ , 6 ▲ , and 3 ▱ .

Take turns.

Try Pick a tile. Fill the puzzle with that number of pattern blocks. Name the shapes that you used. Keep your tile. Remove the pattern blocks. Repeat until each player gets four turns.

Add the numbers on your tiles. The player with the greater sum wins.

Try Again Put the tiles back in the 🛍. Repeat the activity.

Helping Hands

Partner
Talk

Share your thinking while you work.

Start 👫 Get 🎲 🎲.
Get these pattern blocks:

2 ⬡ , 4 ⬟ , 12 ▲ , and 3 ▱ .

Work together.

Try Toss the 🎲 🎲. Look at the number of dots.
Fill the puzzle with that number of pattern blocks.
Put in or take out shapes as you work together
to solve the puzzle.

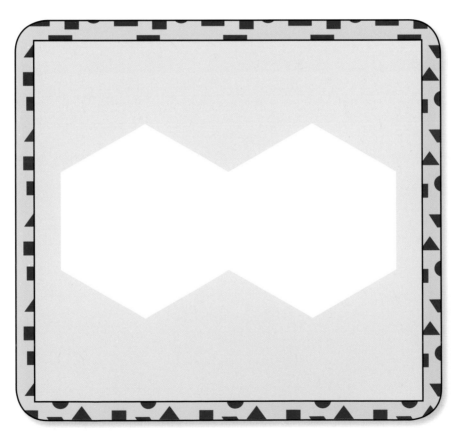

Name each shape in the puzzle.
Remove the pattern blocks.

Try Again Repeat for 5 or more rounds.

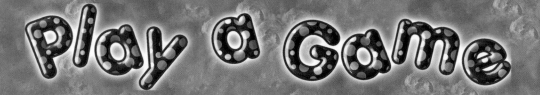

Partner Talk

Share your thinking while you work.

Start 🧑 Get a 🎲 . Get 18 red squares.
Give one game board to each player. Take turns.

Try Toss the 🎲 . Read and follow the directions.

⚀	Cover a sphere.
⚁	Cover a cone.
⚂	Cover a cube.

⚃	Cover a rectangular prism.
⚄	Cover a cylinder.
⚅	Cover any solid figure.

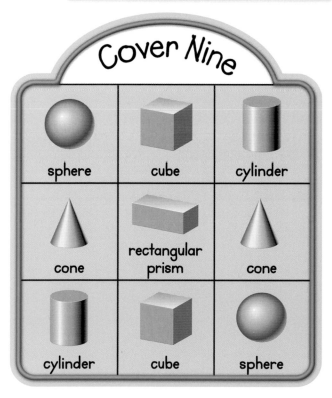

To win, be the first player to cover nine game spaces.

Try Again Play again!

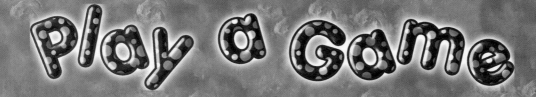

Start  Get a 🎲 . Get 18 red squares.
Give one game board to each player. Take turns.

Try Toss the 🎲 . Read and follow the directions.

⚀	Say and cover the name of a cone.
⚁	Say and cover the name of a sphere.
⚂	Say and cover the name of a cube.

⚃	Say and cover the name of a rectangular prism.
⚄	Say and cover the name of a cylinder.
⚅	Say and cover the name of any solid figure.

Cover Nine

rectangular prism	sphere	cube
cone	cylinder	rectangular prism
cube	cone	sphere

Cover Nine

sphere	cylinder	cone
cone	rectangular prism	sphere
cube	sphere	cylinder

To win, be the first player to cover nine game spaces.

Try Again Play again!

Listen and Learn

Start Put 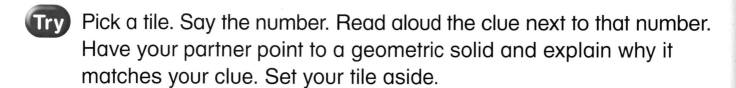 in a .

Take turns.

Try Pick a tile. Say the number. Read aloud the clue next to that number. Have your partner point to a geometric solid and explain why it matches your clue. Set your tile aside.

1. This solid has only 1 flat surface.

2. This solid has only 2 flat surfaces.

3. This solid has no flat surfaces.

4. This solid rolls.

5. This solid has 6 faces.

6. This solid has 8 vertices.

7. This solid has 8 corners.

8. This solid has 6 flat surfaces.

9. This solid does not roll.

a cube

b cone

c sphere

d cylinder

e  rectangular prism

Try Again Repeat until the is empty.
Put the tiles back in the . Repeat the activity.

Listen and Learn

Start Get 9 squares. Get a  . Work together.

Try Put the under the name of a solid.

a
rectangular rism

b
cylinder

c
cone

d
sphere

e
cube

Put a square next to every clue that matches that solid.

1. The solid does not roll.

2. The solid rolls.

3. The solid has only one flat surface.

4. The solid has only two flat surfaces.

5. The solid has 6 flat surfaces.

6. The solid has 8 vertices.

7. The solid has no flat surfaces.

8. The solid has 8 corners.

9. The solid has 1 vertex.

Try Again Repeat the activity for every solid figure.

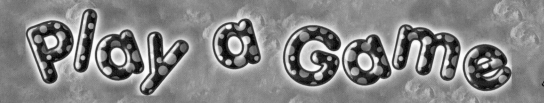

Partner Talk

Share your thinking while you work.

Start 🚶 Get 12 red squares.
Cover each game space with a square. Take turns.

Try Uncover two game spaces.

If you see two solids that roll, or two solids that do not roll, keep the squares.

If not, put the squares back where they were.

Take turns until all the spaces are uncovered.

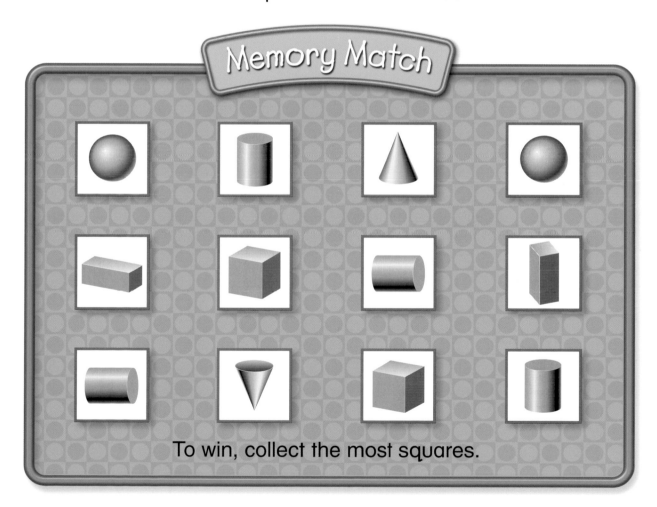

Memory Match

To win, collect the most squares.

Try Again Play again!

Play a Game

Start 👫 Get 12 red squares.
Cover each game space with a square. Take turns.

Try Uncover two game spaces.
Do you see two solids with the same number of flat surfaces?

If you do, tell how many flat surfaces are on each solid. Keep the squares.

If not, put the squares back where they were.

Take turns until all the spaces are uncovered.

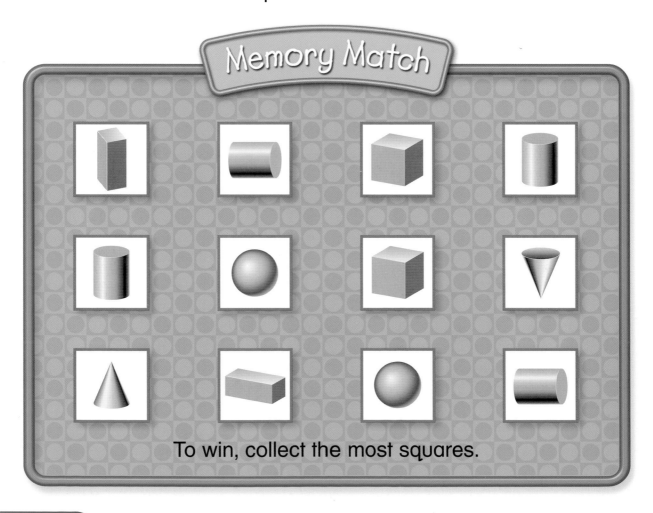

Memory Match

To win, collect the most squares.

Try Again Play again!

Math in Motion

Start 🚶 Practice! Trace each solid figure in the air.
Now take turns. Work together.

SOLID FIGURES

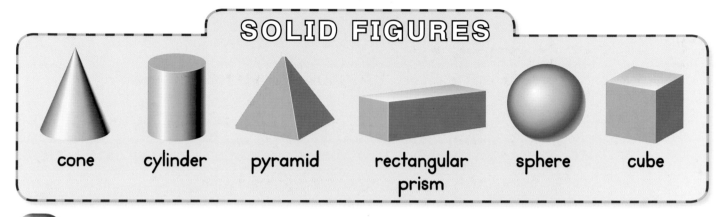

cone   cylinder   pyramid   rectangular prism   sphere   cube

Try Point to a building. Talk about the solid figures it has.
Pretend to make the building by tracing its solid figures with
your finger. Name each solid figure as you trace it.
Work together until you try every building.

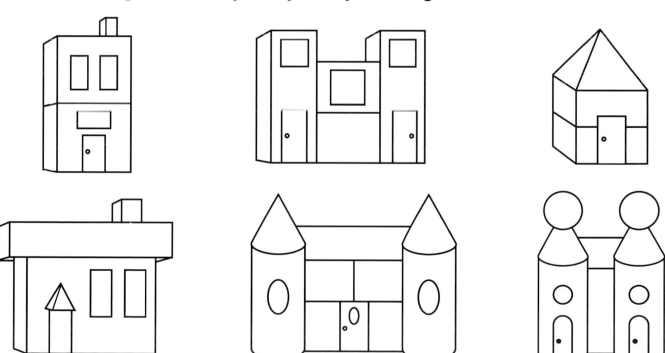

Try Again This time, imagine a different kind of building to trace.
Tell your partner about its solid figures.

Math in Motion

Partner Talk
Share your thinking while you work.

Start  Put ⬜1 ⬜2 ⬜3 ⬜4 ⬜5 ⬜6 in a 🛍.

Practice! Trace each solid figure in the air. Now take turns.

Try Pick a number tile. Find and read your sentences.
Tell your partner what you will make.
Trace your solid figures in the air.
Name each solid figure as you trace it.
Take turns until the of tiles is empty.

SOLID FIGURES

 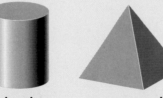

cone   cylinder   pyramid   rectangular prism   sphere   cube

 1 You have a cone and a cylinder. What can you make?

2 You have a cube and a pyramid. What can you make?

3 You have 2 cylinders, 1 pyramid, and 2 cubes. What can you make?

4 You have 3 cylinders, 1 cone, and 2 pyramids. What can you make?

 5 You want to build a robot. Which solid figures will you use?

6 You want to build a castle. Which solid figures will you use?

Try Again Put the tiles back in the 🛍. Play again!

Look and See

Partner Talk
Share your thinking while you work.

Start 👫 Get 2 📎.
Take turns.

Try Put a paper clip over all the cones. Read the questions. Name the questions that helped you find the cones.

Cone   Cylinder   Cube

Clues: How many flat surfaces do I have? What color am I?
How many vertices do I have? Do I roll?
Where am I on the page?

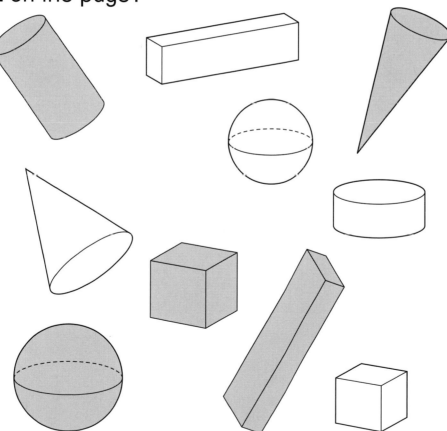

Try Again This time find all the cylinders. Did you use the same questions to find the cylinders and the cones? Why?

Look and See

Start 🏃 Get 2 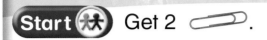.

Try Put a ⬭ over all the spheres. Read the questions.
Name the questions that helped you find the spheres.

Cone   Cylinder   Cube

Clues: How many flat surfaces do I have? What color am I?
How many vertices do I have? Do I roll?
Where am I on the page? Am I a solid figure?

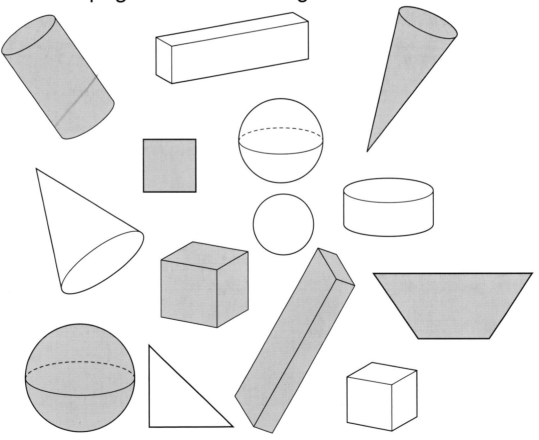

Try Again This time find all the squares. Did you use the same
questions to find the squares and the spheres? Which
questions did you **not** need to use? Why?

Look and See

Start 👫 Put  in a 🛍️ .

Get 10 red squares. Take turns.

Try Pick a tile.

If you choose , look for a pizza that shows 2 equal parts.

If you choose , look for a pizza that shows 4 equal parts.

Explain your answer. Cover that pizza. Put the tile in the 🛍️ .
Play until every pizza showing 2 or 4 equal parts is covered.

Try Again Play again!
Tell how you know that two parts of a pizza are not equal.

Look and See

Partner Talk

Share your thinking while you work.

Start 👥 Get one 🎲. Get 10 red squares. Take turns.

Try Toss the 🎲 to see how many children will share a pizza.

If you toss ⚀, toss again.

Have your partner point to a pizza that has the equal parts the children need. Use a square to cover that pizza. Play until every pizza is covered.

Try Again Play again! Tell how you know that a pizza has equal parts.

Cover Three

Partner Talk

Share your thinking while you work.

Start 👥 Put ⎡2⎤ ⎡2⎤ ⎡2⎤ ⎡4⎤ ⎡4⎤ ⎡4⎤ in a 🛍️.

Get 6 red squares. Get 6 blue squares. Take turns.

Try Pick a tile. Look for a shape that has that number of equal parts. Tell what part of that shape is shaded by completing this sentence: _____ out of _____ equal parts is (or are) shaded. Cover that shape with a square. Put the tile in the 🛍️.

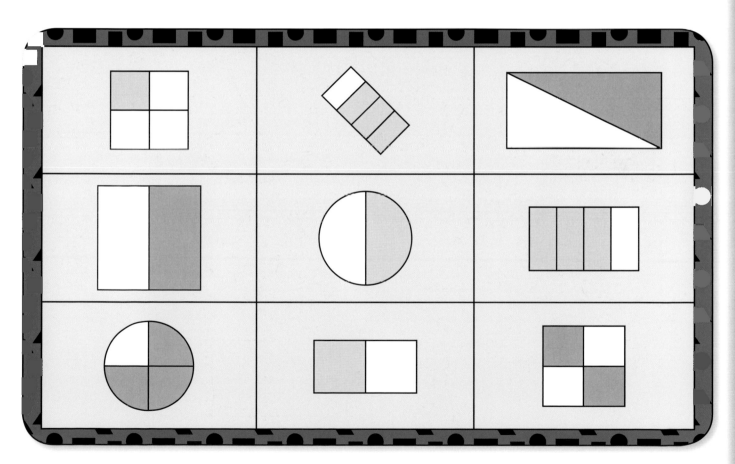

To win, get: ■ ■ ■ or ■ or ■ or ■

Try Again Play again!

Cover Three

Start 👥 Put [2] [2] [2] [4] [4] [4] in a 🛍.

Get 6 red squares. Get 6 blue squares. Take turns.

Try Pick a tile. Look for a shape that has that number of equal parts. Tell what part of that shape is shaded by completing this sentence: _____ out of _____ parts is (or are) shaded. Cover that shape with a square. Put the tile in the 🛍.

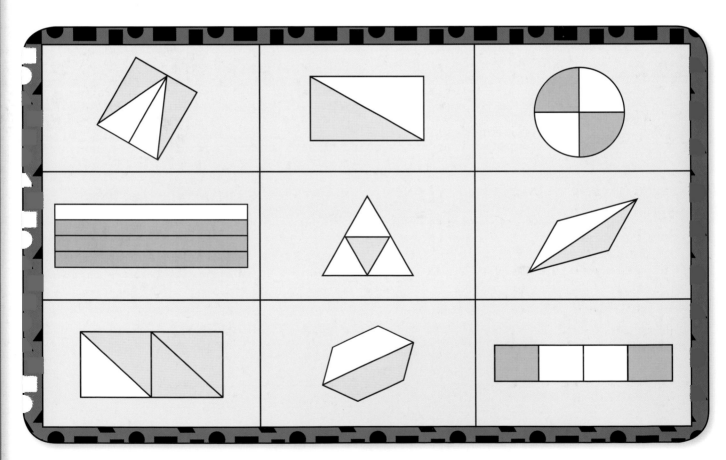

To win, get: ■■■ or ■ or ■ or ■
■ ■ ■
■ ■ ■

Try Again Play again!

Try Together

Partner Talk

Share your thinking while you work.

Start 🏃 Get 4 blue squares.
Get 4 red squares.
Take turns.

Try Point to a letter.
Fill each space with a blue square or a red square.
Ask the question above the workmat.
Let your partner point to and say the answer.

What part of the square is red?

One half	One fourth	One whole	No part

a

red	red
red	red

b

blue	red
blue	red

c

blue	blue
blue	red

d

blue	blue
blue	blue

Try Again This time, tell which square is half blue and which square is a whole blue square.

Try Together

Partner Talk

Share your thinking while you work.

Start   Get 8 blue squares. Get 8 red squares. Take turns.

Try Fill the squares below with some red squares and some blue squares. Ask your partner to follow the directions at the bottom of the workmat.

a

b

c

d

Tell if squares a, b, c, or d are true for one of the following sentences:

One fourth of the square is blue.

One half of the square is blue.

Try Again This time, see if the sentences are true for red.

Look and See

Partner Talk
Share your thinking while you work.

Start 👥 Get one 🎲.
Take turns until each player gets 5 turns.

Try Toss the 🎲.
Match it with a picture.
Tell what part of the shape is grey.

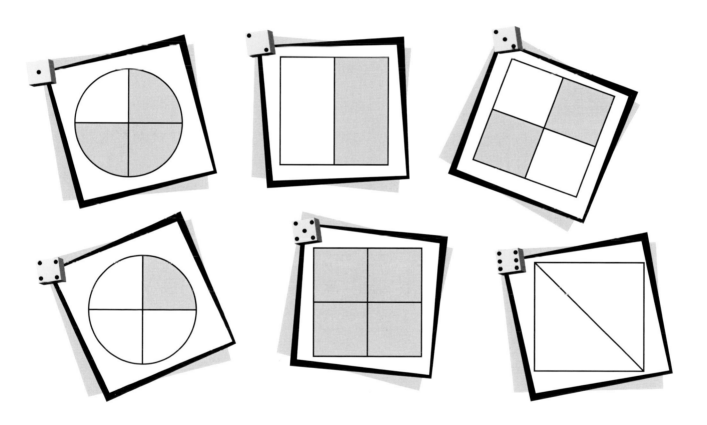

Say: _____ out of _____ .

Try Again This time, describe the part of the shape that is not grey.

Look and See

Start Get one .
Take turns until each player gets 5 turns.

Try Toss the .
Match the number with a sentence.
Read that sentence to your partner.
Tell what part of the shape is gray.
Ask your partner to point to the picture that matches your sentence.

•	1 out of 2 are grey.	::	3 out of 4 are grey.
••	3 out of 5 are grey.	••••	2 out of 5 are grey.
•••	3 out of 6 are grey.	:::	4 out of 5 are grey.

Try Again This time, point to a picture. Ask your partner to read the sentence that describes your picture.